Episcopal Etiquette and Ethics

116 "broken glass of their vows"

EPISCOPAL ETIQUETTE AND ETHICS

Living the Craft of Priesthood in the Episcopal Church

Barney Hawkins

Morehouse Publishing
NEW YORK · HARRISBURG · DENVER

Morehouse Publishing, 4775 Linglestown Road, Harrisburg, PA 17112
Morehouse Publishing, 445 Fifth Avenue, New York, NY 10016
Morehouse Publishing is an imprint of Church Publishing Incorporated.
www.churchpublishing.org

Cover design by Laurie Klein Westhafer
Typeset by Vicki K. Black

Library of Congress Cataloging-in-Publication Data
Hawkins, J. Barney (James Barney)
Episcopal etiquette and ethics : living the craft of priesthood in the Episcopal Church / Barney Hawkins.
    p.   cm.
Includes bibliographical references.
ISBN 978-0-8192-2406-4 (pbk. : alk. paper) 1. Pastoral theology—Episcopal Church. 2. Pastoral theology—Anglican Communion. 3. Priesthood—Episcopal Church. 4. Priesthood—Anglican Communion. 5. Episcopal Church—Clergy—Professional ethics. 6. Anglican Communion—Clergy—Professional ethics. I. Title.
    BV4011.3.H37 2012
    262'.14373—dc23

                                                        2012003614

Printed in the United States of America

10 9 8 7 6 5 4 3 2 1

Contents

Acknowledgments

Imagine Jesus and the disciples without Mary Magdalene. While there is much mystery about their relationship, we can assume that at a very practical level she managed their money and organized their lives. Jesus and his male disciples needed her a great deal. My wife, the Reverend Linda Wofford Hawkins, is as critical to my stability and balance as Mary Magdalene may have been to Jesus and his inner circle. She is a loving life partner who has listened patiently and spoken wisely. Her first-rate mind and deep faith have given texture and proportion to my life and thought. Thanks be to her for ever so much.

In the course of writing these reflections on the priesthood I have used the sermons and remembered the people from parishes I have served as a priest. I could just as easily have given background for my "good priestly habits" by telling stories of life with my precious children, Ellen and Crawford. They are as different as night and day, but both are living accomplished adult lives. They have a father who adores them and is inspired by them. The love Linda and I share is best expressed in the children who have graced our days and given meaning to our lives.

There have been so many mentors in my life I cannot acknowledge them all. Some of them appear in my recollections here. These ardent spirits, including my parents, have believed

in me and called out of me the very image of God, the beloved
child of God that I really am. These mentors have taught me
about love and forgiveness; about art and beauty; about the
ideas and thoughts which will endure; about writing thank you
notes in a timely way and giving small gifts to hosts who welcome me. These mentors—spiritual giants in the landscape of
my life—have made gentle the rugged course of my earthly
journey. I am truly grateful for the communion of mentors I
have been given.

The title of this book is a gift from the Very Reverend Ian
S. Markham, Ph.D., my colleague and the dean and president
of Virginia Theological Seminary. In fact, he suggested an early
outline which gave me a lot to think about. My co-workers in
Institutional Advancement at the seminary have encouraged
me to write and have often shielded me from the interruptions
that are my real job. When not writing in my seminary office,
I have found inspiration in the beauty and remoteness of our
mountain place at Caesar's Head in the northwest corner of
South Carolina. Kanuga Conference Center is nearby, and my
friends there have often provided me with a computer and an
office to think and write, for which I am deeply grateful.

I am very indebted to my students at VTS from the last ten
or so years. They have asked good questions and kept lively
my theological reflection. My three decades of living the craft
of priesthood provide the primary text for my teaching and for
my writing. Teaching is a great joy, and students who learn on
the seminary's Holy Hill inspire me and make me quite hopeful
about the future of the Episcopal Church. The craft that has
been the forge of my life is being passed on to able and faithful
leaders who, God willing, will be priests with good habits. My
students know that the church still matters and that the church
does work that no other institution can do. My co-learners are
ready and willing to be leaders in a church that is and will be
until the end of the ages.

My deep gratitude also is extended to Church Publishing,
especially to Davis Perkins, Nancy Bryan, Vicki Black, and

Ryan Masteller. They have been patient and wise co-workers with me on this project.

This book is dedicated to the faithful who served with me in parish ministry. Trinity Church, Asheville, North Carolina, will always be home base. I was ordained deacon and priest before the parish's great marble altar, and its flock loved me through so many firsts—the birth of our first child, my first celebration of the Holy Eucharist, my first clumsy baptism when the baby pulled my glasses off, my first anxious wedding, my first funeral.

My priesthood began at Trinity but I learned the ropes, if you will, at the Episcopal Church of the Ascension in Hickory, North Carolina. It has been my experience that until you are a rector, you do not understand fully some of the aspects of priesthood. You can observe a vestry meeting until the cows come home. When you are the rector, it is a very different matter. Over almost fourteen years, Ascension helped me become the priest I am. Together, priest and parish, we found our way and lived together with amazing effectiveness and creativity. It was a fruitful, shared ministry. For all practical purposes, Linda and I raised our children in Hickory. If Trinity is my spiritual home base, Ascension will always seem like home for my family.

At the Church of the Redeemer in Baltimore, I was challenged as a seasoned priest. I followed a gifted man who served long and well for almost thirty years. An interim did a lot of the work necessary after such a long tenure. I am grateful to Redeemer for calling out of me new and satisfying administrative and leadership skills. My time in Baltimore at Redeemer was short: only five years. But those years and my ministry in Redeemer stretched me and left on my soul a lasting impression. Redeemer rounded out the parish formation I think I needed in order to teach at Virginia Theological Seminary.

These three parishes—Trinity, Ascension, and Redeemer—have shaped me as the priest I am. Surely it is true: a bishop made me a priest by God's grace, but congregations have confirmed and validated that holy moment. So, I dedicate this book to these three congregations, very different places but so alike in the faithful who find God in these parish families.

— James Barney Hawkins IV
Epiphany 2012

Introduction

Have you ever thought about what you would like to have written on your tombstone? If I were to have an old-fashioned tombstone, I would like my name and only one word: PRIEST. Being a priest has defined my adult life both personally and professionally. Being a priest is engraved on my very being. I really think God made me to be a priest. It is my authentic, true calling. Could I have been a lawyer? Perhaps. Could I have been a banker? Yes, I guess. But being a priest has claimed fully my whole being and all my gifts and talents. All of me has been used up in the craft of priesthood.

This book comes out of my calling and life experience, particularly in the courses I have been teaching for the last twelve years at Virginia Theological Seminary. In 2000 I stepped out of twenty-one years of day-to-day leadership in parish ministry to become the director of the seminary's Doctor of Ministry program. That was my focus until 2007, when I was appointed the seminary's Associate Dean for the Center for Anglican Communion Studies. In 2008 I was given additional duties as the Vice President for Institutional Advancement. In addition to administrative positions, I have also been a member of the teaching faculty as Professor of Pastoral Theology. In class and on campus, I have found myself as one of the go-to persons for students looking for answers to their theological and practical questions about being a priest in today's church. I have sifted through my lecture notes and attempted to remember conversations with students in the past decade to shape the text of *Episcopal Etiquette and Ethics: Living the Craft of Priesthood in the Episcopal Church.*

Women and men come to seminary with questions and leave seminary with questions. It would be tempting to say that their questions are either theological or practical in nature. For me that is an artificial and unhelpful divide. The questions are both/and. By being both theological and practical in scope, the questions reveal themselves to be deeply rooted in the identity of priesthood and in the essence of leadership. What the craft of priesthood looks like for men may not be what it looks like for women. It goes without saying: my vantage point is limited by a number of realities.

Here are some of the questions which recur with slight variations:

- Will being a priest make me different?

- When ordained a priest, am I still a deacon and a member of the laity?

- When celebrating the Holy Eucharist, should I always wear a chasuble? What do I do with my hands when celebrating?

- May I perform private baptisms? Do I wear a white stole as baptizer?

- Should teenagers be confirmed?

- A couple wishes to use the Rolling Stones' "Let's Spend the Night Together" as the entrance music for their wedding: Is that okay?

- Can people get married during Lent?

- Is there such a thing as private confession and absolution in the Episcopal Church?

- Do we believe in "Last Rites"?

- Is it permitted to hold a funeral on Good Friday?

- Does asking people for money have to be part of my ministry?

- Do I need a spiritual director while in seminary? What about a spiritual director after seminary?

- When should I wear a clerical collar?

- Is it all right to bless the food at a wedding banquet with a gin and tonic in my hand?

Some of these questions are very serious; and, yes, some of these questions seem almost trivial. In response to some of the questions, it would be tempting to say—and I often have: please just use some common sense! Yet, some of the most trivial questions are at the heart of the priestly craft. I have concluded that all of these questions and others like them have both a theological and a practical side. This book answers some of these questions for those who are preparing to serve the Episcopal "tribe." It is also for those who are serving and who think often about theology and practice, thought and action, content and appearance, ethics and etiquette in a branch of Christendom that cares a great deal about the interior and exterior Christian life.

At another level, this book is a personal reflection on the meaning and nature of the holy craft of priesthood. A vocation, indeed a call from God which has been acknowledged by the church, stands behind the questions, our theological reflections, and their practical applications. So, the craft of priesthood is about the exterior habit or habits and also the priest's interior spiritual life.

For a number of years I taught, with two colleagues, a course for senior seminarians called "Money, Ministry, and Management." At its core, this course recognized that priesthood is complex and always about managing people—those paid and those who volunteer. It is also about managing money or the allocating of resources. This course taught me that if a priest is to be effective at the altar or in the pulpit, he or she must be an effective leader with the vestry and in the office Monday through Friday. The ministry of administrating is as important as the ministry of presiding or preaching. There is not one "habit" for priesthood. The craft requires many habits, multitasking, and considerable ingenuity.

Other courses have informed my reflections, including a course I taught, again with another faculty colleague, which examined theology and mission in the world. Ministry and mission go together, like a horse and carriage. This course helped seminarians connect the dots: ministry and mission are interwoven in the craft of priesthood. Ministry can never be a domestic craft. We cannot "do" church and forget the world. God's mission in the world must be at the heart of ministry. Archbishop William Temple rightly observed that the church exists primarily for those who are not within its walls. The church is unique in this regard.

A course in preaching allowed me to deal with the pastoral side of proclamation and ways of dealing with difficult texts. But the course which has most informed this book is one taken by a number of our seniors: "The Habit of Priesthood," with a nod to the seventeenth-century Anglican divine George Herbert. *Episcopal Etiquette and Ethics: Living the Craft of Priesthood in the Episcopal Church* is not a research project. The primary text that has informed my seminary teaching is fundamentally my own practice of ministry. Reading in the field has deepened my theological reflection, but my own ministry is the primary text for this book, as it has been for my seminary courses. Unpacking that ministry as a "case study" makes this a memoir of sorts, a reflection both personal and public—for ministry is both.

It is now commonplace to stress the importance of "enculturation" in ministry. A person does not venture out into the mission field or a cross-cultural experience without understanding the culture into which he or she is going. What is true abroad is also true at home. To be effective, we need to relate appropriately to the culture we are serving. The Episcopal

Church is a distinctive culture or "tribe": effective ministry requires an understanding of the distinctive Episcopal culture, which is tradition-rooted, yet ever changing. I will examine unspoken and spoken expectations of priests. I will give ample time to attire, manners, and etiquette, but my reflections are actually more about the deep connections between who we are and what we do and say as priests. Hence, I am focused on the ethics of ministry, if you will. *What does it mean to live an exemplary life in a changing church and world?* The culture of the Episcopal Church has changed dramatically during my three decades of living the craft of priesthood. Many of us would agree that it was a culture which needed change. When I was ordained a priest in 1980, the Episcopal Church was largely white, often rich, and frequently privileged. There was a book in the 1980s that referred to the Episcopal Church's "power and glory." Evangelism was a dirty word. If you did not know where the Episcopal Church was, then you did not belong in it. Women were denied ordination as priests until 1976. In the late twentieth century, Black congregations were small and often without resources. Sociologists of religion could easily chronicle radical shifts in a well-established church that was changing before our eyes.

It is sometimes said that in the Episcopal Church we care about the life of the mind as well as the life of faith. We are a faith tradition that lives out of scripture and tradition, even as both are held up to reason and experience. We are a branch of Christendom which cares about the physical world. Ours is a faith embodied and incarnate. In these pages I take seriously the practical implications of living in the world and not apart from it. So, I take seriously the life of the mind, the life of faith, and the life of practices. But taking seriously the life of the mind puts me somewhat at odds with the Episcopal Church I encounter in 2012. With the social and cultural changes that have rushed across the Episcopal Church in the last decades, do we care as much about the life of mind as once we did? Is the faith we claim as reasonable as it once was? Is the Episcopal Church as educated as it once was? Are Episcopal clergy as well-educated as they were in the last years of the nineteenth century and the early years of the twentieth? The contextual and cultural reality of the Episcopal Church is complex. We are a "tribe" which holds in tension faith and reason, heart and mind. We are still largely white, but while there was a time when the Episcopal Church could be described as well-educated and upper class, today we are more middle class. As society has changed and become more diverse, so has the Episcopal Church. This has meant a painful but necessary transition. Class and privilege have been challenged by work and service. The ministry of the baptized has dethroned the ministry dominated by the ordained. No longer is there a "Father knows best" world in the Episcopal Church. Today's clergy need updated preparation and new skills for ministry.

I have been ordained for thirty-three years. No guidebook for being an effective priest was presented to me by my ordaining bishop in 1979—and had it been given to me, it would be out-of-date today. There was no manual of best practices, to employ an overused phrase that I do not fully understand. There were books about priesthood, but I had to find them on my own. In 1979 almost nothing was said about mentoring or training. Priesthood was conferred with only the theological directions contained in the *Book of Common Prayer*. Practical directions were assumed to be part of "on-the-job training." The craft was learned not taught. How does the Episcopal Church shape men and women for the craft of priesthood today? Is order in the ranks necessary or desirable? This book is published in a time of crisis within the Episcopal Church, a crisis that has been brewing for decades. Three-year residential seminary education for ordained leadership is being questioned and is under revision. A number of new models for education and formation have arisen. New priests and seasoned priests, however, will always need mentors, guidebooks, and careful theological reflection if today's congregations and church institutions are to have effective, thoughtful leadership. Our leaders must be shaped for the craft of priesthood. It cannot be left to chance.

The first chapter is a memoir of my path to Holy Orders and my craft of priesthood in four distinct settings. This overview gives a summative text from which I draw for theological reflection on the practice of ministry, which makes up the rest of the book. I have found it necessary to reflect theologically and to remember carefully the people and places of my ministry. My priesthood is worn with particular people and places in mind, and this particularity profoundly shapes the "etiquette and ethics" of my leadership and priesthood in the Episcopal Church.

To be honest, I wish I could be more detached. It would be easier to treat priesthood as an abstract vocation. In the decade before I actively began my journey to priesthood, I read *Markings,* published in 1964 by Dag Hammarskjöld. His life of public service "required a sacrifice of all personal interests," so Hammarskjöld wrote for Edward Murrow's radio program.[1] *Markings* is silent about the historical events of his time and devoid of references to his career and the people he encountered. In his iconic book, Hammarskjöld tells the story of being more and more present to his neighbor as he lived fully and painfully with his own frailties and ambiguity. The book spoke loudly to me while I was in college. What Hammarskjöld omitted has become quite necessary for me as I think of my ministry—a ministry of serving God and others, a ministry of "personal interests," a ministry shaped by God and all the people I have encountered.

Most of this book is organized with the sacraments as guideposts and through the prism of the pastoral offices. It is a pilgrimage through the priestly craft of effective and faithful service, from the inner life of prayer to outward attire. It is a literary pilgrimage of sorts that is informed by the Bible, the *Book of Common Prayer,* writers, poets, and the saints (past and present) in congregations and communities who have shaped me as a priest. It is a guidebook comprised of my theological reflections on priesthood for anyone who wants to serve as a priest in God's church. It may be ideal reading for

---

1. Edward R. Murrow's interview with Dag Hammarskjöld in November 1953 can be heard at http://thisIbelieve.org/essay/16608/.

those who share ministry with the ordained. This book is an invitation to lay and ordained leaders to reflect theologically on the ministry we share; on that which we read, hear, say and do; on the persons we meet in ministry; on our own being and "personal interests"; and on the vocation which is ours in Christ Jesus our Lord. As the "priesthood of all believers," the whole church lives the craft of priesthood. I am looking closely at the particularity of priesthood which belongs to those ordained priests—for the sake of the church's life, ministry, and mission.

Chapter 1

A Case Study

Being a priest has been worth my life.

M y path to Holy Orders and my life as a priest is uniquely mine. I offer my path as a "case" in ministry, as the context for my theological reflection on ministry practices. I have reflected upon my priestly formation and tried to make sense of the difficult path it was. To me now, the path to Holy Orders was as important as priesthood itself, the journey as critical as the destination. The craft of priesthood was forged in a fire, "always burning but never consuming," in the words of Catherine of Siena.

Let me begin with my baptism. I grew up in the northwest corner of South Carolina. The church nearest to the small farm on which I lived was Reedy River Baptist Church. It was there in a chilly tank of water that I was "dunked" three times with the ancient words: "I baptize you in the name of the Father, and of the Son, and of the Holy Spirit." I was told that I was "born again" and I believed the preacher. In her short story "The River," Flannery O'Connor tells of a river baptism at which the preacher said to the one being baptized: "You count now. You did not even count before." When I was baptized at age nine, I really believed that I counted. It was a serious passage for me, but I soon forgot my new identity and went on with my life much the same as before. My baptism did not cross my mind in my high school years. I had other fish to fry.

In college I felt the "nudging" that often goes with the call to priesthood. At Furman University, across the road from my childhood home, I encountered the Reverend L. D. Johnson, who was the university's chaplain. He was the first real liberal in my conservative life. In 1968 he talked about pacifism and the role of women in the church's leadership. He looked beyond the color of a person's skin to the image of God deep within. He was the first person I ever heard speak of gays and lesbians with dignity and affection. He had a prophetic voice that stood squarely in the face of the powers and principalities of this world, and in his case that would have included the hierarchy of the Southern Baptist Church. If baptism got me thinking for awhile about God and my life, Chaplain Johnson's mentoring of me became the second great passage for me, a passage in which I was searching for what I would do with my life.

Because of a liberal Baptist chaplain at a university that was differentiating itself from the narrow-minded Southern Baptist Church (the monolith that hovered over the whole of the South in those days), I found the Episcopal Church. I told the chaplain that I did not feel at home in the church of my baptism. It was too stark. There was too much talk of sin and hell. Dr. Johnson said, "You must visit Christ Church downtown." I visited Christ Church the first time on Christmas Eve. I could not believe the pomp and ceremony, the vestments, the grandeur. I listened to and liked the sermon. I could not miss the mystery of Holy Communion. Perhaps for all the wrong reasons, I fell in love with the Episcopal Church—and through the liturgy I came to the deep well which is Anglican theology.

Through Dr. Johnson's encouragement, I entered Duke Divinity School. Linda Dell Wofford and I married in 1975, both of us discerning a call to the priesthood—a very difficult thing for women at that time! Linda entered the Divinity School at Duke as I took graduate courses and pondered my future. Linda's faith and courage in beginning her theological training with no assurance that the craft of priesthood would ever be opened to women in the Episcopal Church was inspiring. Settling once again into an academic life was made quite complex by my decision to pursue Holy Orders in the Episcopal Church. As a graduate student at Duke, my life was increasingly shaped by my ministry as the Lay Pastoral Assistant at St. Philip's, Durham. I preached often, read more and more Anglican theology, and got to know a cast of caring priests who became important conversation partners as I began a formal path to Holy Orders.

The year 1976 was a confusing time in the Episcopal Church. We were finding our way through a long revision of the *Book of Common Prayer*. There was a listening process about the ordination of women to the priesthood, an issue which had polarized the church. The prior decades had been a bewildering season for mainline churches as the civil rights movement traveled blood-stained streets in many American cities. The Vietnam War divided the country and left us uncertain about the future. The Episcopal Church mirrored the world's conflict and chaos. The cultural changes experienced by the Episcopal Church were not always the church's own choosing. Social change was momentous and the church was shaken loose from her moorings. It is sad to assert, but the Episcopal Church did not lead the way in civil rights or women's rights. The church reacted more than it acted. Of course, there were clarion prophets along the way: John Hines, Verna Dozier, and John Walker, to name just three. But for the most part, the Episcopal Church protected the status quo. If the church was unsure about its own identity and role, so much more was the case for Episcopal priests. In the period between 1960 and 1980, priests went from being highly esteemed in their congregations and communities to being almost without portfolio in the same bailiwicks. The civil rights movement and the Vietnam War tore at the fabric of the well-established Episcopal Church. The craft of priesthood was under construction—and many were overly cautious about those claiming a call or discerning a vocation. For would-be ordinands, suspicion was as common a response as affirmation.

So my years of seminary education took place in the midst of tumultuous change in the Episcopal Church. The path to Holy Orders ended for me in the Diocese of Western North Carolina. St. Luke's in Boone became my sponsoring parish, and I was ordained a deacon at a diocesan service held at my new parish, Trinity Church in Asheville, in the summer of 1979. My family and Linda's family were part of the service, though oddly, I remember very little about it. As strange as it may seem, I remember best the deep blue carpet upon which I knelt. The day after, I served as deacon at the high marble altar for the two Sunday services. I had trouble getting my stole pinned and over the correct shoulder. I retreated to my office at one point that Sunday to read the unframed ordination certificate on my desk. Above the episcopal shield of Bishop Weinhauer, which was set in red wax on a purple ribbon, were the words that the bishop did "ordain as Deacon in the Protestant Episcopal Church in the United States of America, our beloved brother in Christ, James Barney Hawkins IV, B.A., M.Div. of whose pious, sober and honest life and conversation, competent learning, knowledge of the Holy Scriptures, and soundness in the Faith we are well assured. . . . " The certificate also noted that in the bishop's and congregation's presence the ordinand "freely and voluntarily declared that he believes the Holy Scriptures, of the Old and New Testaments to be the Word of GOD, and to contain all things necessary to Salvation; and having solemnly sworn to conform to the Doctrine, Discipline and Worship of the Church. . . . " I tried to take in the description of me as "pious, sober, and honest." Did I possess "competent learning"? What about "soundness in the Faith"? I marveled at what I had "declared" about the Bible. I was perplexed by my oath to "conform to the Doctrine, Discipline and Worship of the Church." I thought: What have I gotten myself into? Is this what I have been praying about for so long? Has the path to Holy Orders brought me to this serious moment?

If St. Luke's, Boone was a mentoring parish, Trinity Church will always be a "home place" for me. I lived so much life in the two years I was there. Trinity is home to us primarily because of the birth of our Ellen. She was born with Down syndrome and our lives were changed forever on July 1, 1980. Linda was thirty years old and there was nothing high risk about the uneventful pregnancy, although Ellen was three weeks late. We were shocked when Linda's childhood friend and our pediatrician told us within hours of her birth that dear Ellen had a congenital condition about which we were unaware. I thought the worst thing that could happen to us had happened. Over the years of our life with Ellen, I have come to see that the day of her birth may have been one of the best days of my blessed life. If I am honest, up to July 1, 1980, my life was totally about me. Ellen's birth changed that—to a certain degree. If the path to Holy Orders had been arduous, I suddenly confronted the biggest challenge of my life.

Ellen is Tuesday's child. I had been a priest for fifty-eight days when she was born. I was scheduled to preside at the Holy Eucharist in Trinity's Redwood Chapel on the Friday following Ellen's birth. My rector and first mentor in my priesthood, the Reverend Grahame Butler-Nixon, offered to assist me as the deacon, and I gratefully accepted. After that simple weekday service with about a dozen of the faithful attending, Grahame said something to me as memorable as the words I heard on the day of my ordination to the priesthood. He quietly observed: "Barney, you truly became a priest today." Of course, we both knew in that tender moment that the press of holy hands and the continuity of apostolic succession mattered on June 30, 1979 and May 3, 1980. But I also knew what Grahame meant. In a holy moment, covered up with sadness and facing an uncertain future, I raised my hands over bread and wine and they became the Body and Blood of our Lord and Savior Jesus Christ. For one brief moment, I knew that I was doing what I was made to do. My priesthood would be worth a life. I was a priest after the Order of Melchizedek and presiding at the altar in Redwood Chapel that day was the important work of my life.

During the years at Trinity, I was carefully shaped as a priest—at the altar and in the pulpit—by my rector. Grahame was precise in his sacramental duties, and he knew well the theology which underpinned every action. After services, he would gently reflect with me on the celebration. He wanted me to "own" my presiding practices. He wanted me to master the craft. Grahame's priesthood was deeply centered in the pastoral offices. If I am a pastor, it is because I learned from one whose priesthood was people-centered because it was God-centered. I found my preaching voice and style in Trinity's pulpit—encouraged by a congregation that listened and affirmed.

Indeed, I got to preach a lot at Trinity. Strangely enough, regular preaching awakened my faith and my love of the Bible. I assume most people in the pew conclude that a lively faith and knowledge of Holy Scripture precede good preaching. But in the regular practice of preaching, I found God (or God found me). My faith became stronger as I served as a deacon and then a priest at the altar, taught in church school, visited the sick, presided at celebrations of marriages, and participated in the reading of the burial office. But it was in preaching that my faith was the most stretched.

At Trinity I did not learn a lot about the intricacies of a parish's administrative life. That was my own fault. I was still not convinced that ministry included administering. I did learn at Trinity what it meant to "conform to the doctrine, discipline and worship of the Church in these United States of America," to quote my ordination certificates. Grahame was a strong patriarchal figure who knew doctrine, respected discipline, and loved the worship of the Episcopal Church. While serving as curate and later associate at Trinity Church, I came to appreciate both the order and discipline of the Episcopal Church. I had always questioned authority; but after ordination, I slowly accepted episcopal oversight and the rector's authority—and in so doing, I think I opened myself for the first time to the rule of God in my life. As my life and ministry were conformed to

the solemn vows of my diaconal and priestly ordinations, I discovered my true relationship with a loving and gracious God.
As a new priest, I learned to accept people, being more about
conversation than conversion. My earliest priestly habits derive
from a theology that has its roots in creation and is grounded
in the goodness of God.

The Church of the Ascension, Hickory

I was thirty-two years old and the Church of the Ascension was
my first rectorship. I had no idea of the work that was ahead
of me! I loved the Celebration of New Ministry, though in
those days it was a service focused more on the priest and less
on the congregation. Mutual ministry was a concept being articulated but not fully formed in the Diocese of Western North
Carolina. By the time I departed Ascension in 1995, the services
celebrating new ministries were about shared ministry, the new
ministry of congregation and leader together. My ordaining
bishop gave me a "letter of institution" as rector of Ascension.
This all seemed rather official. I will never forget the comment
at the door after the service celebrating "my" new ministry:
"You will please everyone here: some the day you come; some
while you are here; and some the day you leave." Much wisdom!

The Church of the Ascension was ready to grow, yet not
ready to change. It was a pastoral-sized church that could not
avoid becoming a program-sized church with substantial resources for ministry. I enjoyed celebrating, preaching, and
teaching. Pastoral care took much of my time, and this soon
became a challenge as the parish grew younger with new members and older with stakeholders who were aging rapidly. I was
not skilled at administering a parish, supervising a staff, or
leading a vestry. So I made many mistakes, even as most of the
congregation forgave me and encouraged me as I continued to
grow into the many roles associated with the craft of priesthood.

At the Church of the Ascension, I developed leadership skills to complement the liturgical and sacramental skills which I discovered while serving at Trinity, Asheville. I learned how to work with a vestry. I was forced to develop fund-raising skills when the vestry and parish decided to purchase a Flentrop organ. I saw at Ascension that the craft of priesthood includes community leadership and community organizing. As a priest serving as a rector, I stepped fully into the all-purpose garment or habit of priesthood. Over and over again, I realized that leadership was also about being a faithful pastor, tending to the myriad needs of a congregation growing and changing. Being at the bedside of the dying gave credibility and depth to my administrative work with the vestry. Working closely with wardens and the lay leadership of Ascension informed and shaped my preaching and teaching. I learned that administration is part of ministry and not an unwelcomed intruder. What the priest does on Tuesday is as important as what the priest does on Sunday.

If I preached mostly about God the Creator, God the Father, while at Trinity, Asheville, my sermons at Ascension were very much focused on Jesus Christ, the second person of the Trinity. For almost fourteen years I preached at least once a week, save the times when I was on vacation. I often taught a course in adult education. Confirmation classes, EYC, and vacation Bible school were part of my brief, even when an associate was on staff. In all the busyness of parish life, I drew consolation and strength primarily from a healing service with the Holy Eucharist and homily every Wednesday afternoon. At first I thought that healing with the laying on of hands was "hocus pocus" and too far off the path of my "reasonable" Christianity. I knew I believed in sacred mystery, but I wondered if the laying on of hands was related to magic. Yet as I laid hands on the heads of the faithful one Wednesday after another, week after week, I became a believer in the power of Jesus to heal memories, bodies, minds, souls, and relationships. I saw with my own eyes that Jesus, the Great Physician, heals and sustains the faithful. I experienced Jesus driving from bodies and minds "all sickness and disease," as we would say in our Prayers of the People. Wednesday's healing service at the Church of the Ascension expanded my relationship with Jesus as my Lord and Savior, my brother and my physician.

My ministry at Ascension was a deeply shared ministry. Early in my time as rector I was reading a lot about mutual ministry, the up and coming "thing." Ascension was beginning to live into the 1979 *Book of Common Prayer,* with its increased emphasis on the ministry of all the baptized. Ascension was growing, and there was the need for more organizational structure and committees. The rector could not be everywhere, so lay leadership was encouraged and it flourished. I remember the day a senior warden said to me: "Well, it's time we focus on Jesus' disciples as well as Jesus." To borrow a phrase from Reynolds Price, it is also important to remember the "ardent spirits," those dear souls who help us live through the cold nights and long days that go with ministry.[2]

The Church of the Redeemer, Baltimore

In the tenth year of my rectorship in Hickory, I became restless and reflective about my ministry at Ascension. A servant leadership workshop led by the Right Reverend Bennett Sims at Kanuga Conference Center in Hendersonville, North Carolina, became a critical moment of discernment for me. For the first time I looked beyond my ministry at Ascension and in Western North Carolina and imagined a new place of service and leadership, a new place to live the craft of priesthood. In the spring of 1994, I began conversations with the search committee charged with finding a rector for the Church of the Redeemer in Baltimore, Maryland, Bishop Sims's former parish. The chair of the search committee was one of the authors of the widely influential book *Listening Hearts: Discerning Call in Community,* and there was a prayerful, spiritual tone to the committee's interaction with me. Discernment had become a dirty word on my path to Holy Orders. Suddenly, discernment took on a new,

---

2. Reynolds Price, *Ardent Spirits: Leaving Home, Coming Back* (New York: Scribner, 2009).

positive meaning. As the months went by, I asked myself: Is this a call or am I fascinated with the size of Redeemer? Or could it be both? Three members of the search committee came to see me in Hickory. We talked over lunch in a booth at Applebee's. They came to services on Sunday at Ascension. I knew that day that I would be going to Baltimore.

In December of 1994, I was called to be the rector of this venerable north Baltimore parish, assuming my duties on Lent IV of 1995. I soon learned that it is not easy to move from a program-size church in a small Southern town to a resource-size church in a major metropolitan area. Quickly, I learned that I wore pastoral garments more easily than the garments required of a corporate rector. After almost fourteen years, I knew the names of everyone in Ascension, Hickory. I soon realized I would never know all of the communicants in the Baltimore parish of some thirty-five hundred members.

The craft of priesthood is always about context. What works in one parish does not necessarily work in another. One "size" of priestly habit does not fit all situations. Context matters more than we think. Reflecting on my five years in Baltimore, I would call it a transitional ministry for me and an extended interim for the parish. I followed a rector who had served the parish with distinction for twenty-nine years. There was an interim, but his work was not completed before I arrived. I left before finishing my work. I never lived fully into my rectorship at the Church of the Redeemer.

The Church of the Redeemer in Baltimore demanded good preaching as no other parish in which I served. I spent more time preparing my sermons in Baltimore than ever before or since. I knew that I had a congregation which expected the best and knew the best when they heard it. It was a challenge to preach the Good News of God in the Holy Trinity and to connect that theology to the real lives of the faithful who called Redeemer their spiritual home. I had a fine staff while serving in Baltimore, and I learned more from them than I knew at the time. This is to say that I was not alone on Sunday mornings.

Others were co-ministers with me and that made all the difference in my craft of priesthood.

Virginia Theological Seminary and Immanuel Church-on-the-Hill

In 2000 I joined the faculty of the Virginia Theological Seminary (VTS) as Director of the Doctor of Ministry Program and Professor of Parish Ministry. It was not an easy transition. I missed congregational preaching. I preached only sporadically in the seminary's chapel, and it was not a felicitous assignment for me. Since chapel was required, I did not trust the congregation, to be blunt. Why were faculty and students really there? I surmised that they might be there to pick apart my sermon.

I missed parish life and the routine of my life for over twenty years. Transitioning from a church calendar to an academic calendar was quite an adjustment. Because of "Christmas break," Christmas came and went on the Holy Hill largely without notice. What do you mean, there are no services on Good Friday? Rather quickly, I put aside the liturgical practice of my priesthood, for all practical purposes. I became somewhat rusty at the craft. My silver home communion set became tarnished and sat on the library shelf, rarely opened.

After about five years at VTS, I was asked to be an Honorary Associate at Immanuel Church-on-the-Hill (ICOH), the congregation so closely connected to the seminary for the last seventy years. Serving as a priest there is very different from being the rector of a parish. At ICOH I am an occasional preacher, but the sermons I have preached at ICOH do not reveal much about my priestly craft. I know and I do not know the congregation. Being an Honorary Associate has taught me that it must be difficult to be a priest without full-time priestly duties. Without a specific ministry, I sometimes feel like an occasional priest. Perhaps I am confessing that the craft of priesthood must be lived day-in and day-out. Priesthood cannot be a hobby. It must be a vocation that consumes all of my life. Over time, I have discovered that teaching is one way of living the craft of priesthood. This has not been an easy lesson to learn.

The path of my ordained ministry—from Trinity Church, Asheville to the Church of the Ascension, Hickory to the Church of the Redeemer, Baltimore to the Virginia Theological Seminary and Immanuel Church—has been a powerful but not very peaceful journey with God. It has also been a difficult theological journey. The geography of my ministry is measured more by my journey with God and the church's creeds than by locating specific cities on a map. Over and over again and with the hope that the "thousandth time would prove the charm," I have recited the church's creeds, Apostles' and Nicene, as I have tried to preach the God of the creeds. In all the congregations I have served I have been honest: I have led and said the creeds because they contain what the church believes. I have not always believed all that the church believes. But reflecting theologically on my ministry, I can assert that it has been a steady walk, line by line through the creeds, as God revealed God's nature to the church and, thankfully, to me. My sermons bear out this learning.

In the exercise of living my life craft or vocation, I have learned more and more about God, God's church, and the priesthood. I have found that preaching has been the best way for me to travel the geography of my ministry and life. Sermons are moments for me that bring together the temporal and the timeless, the place where I engage the creeds and the great faith statements of our tradition.

My sermons connect me to people and places, and the very heart of my priesthood. And yet preaching is not the refiner's fire of my priesthood. Standing at the altar as presider has always been the great tutorial for me. The altar has been my office. It is the place of my holy work and the source from which all my work has flowed. It was Thomas Cranmer who so beautifully connected the Holy Eucharist to the very nature of God and the church. He wrote:

> For like as bread is made of a great number of grains of corn, ground, baken, and so joined together, that thereof is made one loaf; and an infinite number of grapes be pressed together in one vessel, and thereof is made wine; likewise is the whole multitude of true Christian people spiritually joined, first to Christ, and then among themselves together in one faith, one baptism, one Holy Spirit, one knot and bond of love.[3]

Thomas Cranmer would have known a Greek text from about AD 110 which was translated for a hymn by F. Bland Tucker: "As grain, once scattered on the hillsides, was in this broken bread made one, so from all lands thy Church be gathered into thy kingdom by thy Son."[4]

Our baptismal theology echoes with the same words of the truth that Cranmer knew. When the church gathers to baptize, the presider says: "There is one Body and one Spirit." The people respond: "There is one hope in God's call to us." The presider confesses: "One Lord, one Faith, one Baptism." And finally, the people say: "One God and Father of all."[5] The opening sentences of the service for Holy Baptism are grounded in the "broken bread made one" and begin with Cranmer's one body, "the whole multitude of true Christian people spiritually joined." The last opening sentence is an affirmation that there is one God.

In the celebration of the Holy Eucharist, the presider and the people of God are silent before the fraction, that moment when the consecrated bread is broken. Countless times I have lifted the "loaf" about which Cranmer wrote—lifted it high for all to see. I believed in that holy moment that this is consecrated bread—that it is the Body of Jesus Christ. This I believe but I do not understand it. The bread is the Body of Christ and by it we have spiritual union with our Lord and Savior. As the Body

3. Thomas Cranmer, "The First Book of the Sacrament," in *The Works of Thomas Cranmer,* ed. J. E. Cox (Cambridge: Parker Society, 1844), 42.
4. *The Hymnal 1982* (New York: Church Hymnal Corporation, 1985), hymn 302.
5. *The Book of Common Prayer* (New York: Church Hymnal Corporation, 1979), 299.

of Christ, the bread, the "loaf," is also the very church that is one with Christ. St. Paul wrote in 1 Corinthians 10:16: "The cup of blessing that we bless, is it not a sharing in the blood of Christ? The bread that we break, is it not a sharing in the body of Christ?" As I lift the bread which is the Body, I also hold within my small hands that "wonderful and sacred mystery" which is the church. It is a holy moment in my sacred priesthood because in one action I lift up Christ for all to see, even as they see themselves as his body. We partake of Christ and in so doing we become what we eat. We are the body of Christ. You are what you eat after all! After a "period of silence is kept," as the Prayer Book rubric urges, the presider says: "Christ our Passover is sacrificed for us." The people answer: "Therefore let us keep the feast."

Keeping the feast is a wonderful metaphor for the craft of priesthood. We eat the bread and we drink the wine, "Food to pilgrims given."[6] As priests, we stand before the "pilgrims" as we labor together with them "to build up the family of God."[7] In the Ordination of a Priest, as part of the Examination, the bishop asks a series of questions. The first is about call: "Do you believe that you are truly called by God and his Church to this priesthood?" The woman or man about to be ordained responds, "I believe I am so called." The bishop then asks, "Do you now in the presence of the Church commit yourself to this trust and responsibility?" To which the ordinand affirms, "I do." A series of questions then follows about having respect for and being guided by the "pastoral direction and leadership of your bishop"; being "diligent in the reading and study of the Holy Scriptures"; ministering the "sacraments of the New Covenant"; being a "faithful pastor"; and seeking to "pattern your life in accordance with the teachings of Christ" and to "persevere in prayer, both in public and in private."[8] Such is the "feast" of the sacred priesthood, and I will return to these themes. Living the craft of priesthood is about engaging such

---

6. *The Hymnal 1982*, hymn 309.
7. *The Book of Common Prayer* (1979), 532.
8. *The Book of Common Prayer* (1979), 531–532.

vows, even as God gives us "the grace and power to perform them."

Keeping the feast is one thing. Serving the feast is quite another. In the following chapters I will invite both lay and ordained readers to think deeply about the craft of priesthood as it is lived out in the daily life of the church. We put on the all-purpose habit of priesthood to serve the feast to the People of God, a feast that is both word and sacrament.

Chapter 2

Coming to the Waters of Holy Baptism

Priests are often asked theological questions for which they have no off-the-cuff answers. Perhaps we should remedy that malady. Since I started living the craft of priesthood in the dark ages before computers, I have file cards on which I jot down ideas, thoughts, questions, and answers. I am thereby somewhat prepared when someone asks me complicated questions like: What is the Holy Eucharist? Why do we call it "Communion"? What does baptism mean? Will we go to hell if we are not baptized? Why do we baptize babies?

It is important to decide what you really believe. I remember sitting in a seminary class when a Doctor of Ministry student said to the professor, "Okay. You have told us what Schleiermacher and Moltmann believe about the problem of evil in the world. Now what do *you* believe about the problem of evil?" The professor found it quite difficult to answer the question. Priests must remember that the people who come to church on Sundays or to a Saturday morning baptismal class are searching—whether they know it or not—for answers to life's hardest questions. It is true that most priests are a work in progress when it comes to their theology, but it seems fair for there to be some expectation that the baptizer have some sense of the sacrament being administered.

So, I suggest that you get an old-fashioned three-by-five card or create a card on the computer. On the card, in four or five sentences, write a brief statement about what you believe about this or that. Having the support of scriptural verses is not a bad idea since so much of the *Book of Common Prayer* is scripture transposed. You will have a number of cards over time as you live the craft of priesthood and offer the church's sacraments. Here is an example. For baptism, you might have a card which says:

> *In the waters of baptism we are buried with Christ in his death and we share in his resurrection. By the Holy Spirit we are cleansed from sin, born again and marked as Christ's own forever. Forever is an important word here: the sacrament of Holy Baptism cannot be voided and we do not re-baptize. The sacrament of Holy Baptism is a life-changing sacrament. We are forever part of the church, the family of God.*

These sentences about baptism are drawn largely from the *Book of Common Prayer*. Or, you might keep a story in mind to help you explain baptism. You could recall that Martin Luther had these words on the wall of his study: "I have been baptized." Why? Did he feel it necessary to keep before him the truth that in his baptism he was one with Christ? Luther believed that baptism bestows an identity and affirms our unity with Christ. It is the beginning of a new way of life. To be washed in the baptismal waters is rather radical. One priest friend of mine told me once that no loving parent in his/her right mind would present a child for baptism. He said, "How can you give a child away? That's what baptism is—you give the child back to God who first gave you the child."

As priest and people draw near to the font, it is a place surely where "the heart of the Eternal is most wonderfully kind."[9] The church of God is never more open and inclusive, never more a blending of heaven and earth, than at baptism, when the priest and people say together: "We receive you into

---

9. "There's a wideness in God's mercy," *The Hymnal 1982*, hymn 469.

the household of God. Confess the faith of Christ crucified, proclaim his resurrection, and share with us in his eternal priesthood."[10] Priest and people are called to receive, to confess, and to share fully in the priesthood of the Eternal Word made flesh, even Jesus our Lord and Savior. Here the church is a priestly ministry, even a priestly minister.

Vignettes of baptism

It is Tuesday afternoon and I receive a phone call. "We will be in town in a few weeks and I want my baby christened. She is so precious. I was christened and married at Ascension, and I love the place. It's so pretty—although my father thinks the new organ is too big and too loud. My mother will be in touch to make all the arrangements, and she wants you to bless the food at the party afterwards. We already have the club reserved. Bye."

A very active couple in the parish asks me to baptize their grandchild at the family home on Martha's Vineyard. They say, "We know about your policy of private baptisms but in August the whole extended family will be with us for about four days. Our dearest friends and yours from the parish will be with us. It just makes sense to do a little service on the porch. I will have a silver bowl engraved for the occasion. We will send the plane down for you. Won't Linda, of course, come with you? What about Ellen? She is such a doll. Would you like to use the guest house for a few days afterwards?"

The classes for baptismal instruction are going well: the parents and godparents for five babies, two teenagers, and one

---

10. *The Book of Common Prayer* (1979), 308.

adult male. After class one evening, the adult male lingers to ask a question. "Do I have to be baptized on Sunday in front of everyone?" I repeat my theological reasons for public baptism instead of private baptism. I say this is such a special time; everyone will be rejoicing with you. He pauses, drops his head, and says: "I just cannot do it." We walk over to my office and for the next two hours he tells me his life story. Coming to Christ as a twenty-eight year old was part of a long, painful journey with family and friends. He had overcome many obstacles. He was accepting himself as a "beloved child of God," but he was still vulnerable and hurting about many things. Prep school had been a nightmare. College was not much better. The more I listen the more I know that his should be a private baptism with two or three special friends.

I am beeped: the new baby we are expecting in the parish was born with many physical challenges. It looks like she will not make it. Her parents plead, please hurry and baptize her at the hospital.

It is Sunday morning at the 9 a.m. service. The family of one of the three children being baptized fills the first two pews on the epistle side. After the baptism and at the Peace, the family in the first two pews walks out, down the center aisle. They had attended the baptismal instruction on Saturday morning, when we "walked through" the service, including Communion. They did not attend services often; perhaps, in their defense, they thought the service was over.

Good priestly habits,
with theological reflections

The first vignette finds me talking with the grandmother, not the mother of the child. This is not the best protocol, but often young married people with babies return home for baptism, perhaps because they are not active in church where they live. I was prepared when the mother called. I arranged for us to meet. We chit-chat and then she says, "The date is set because I was so lucky to get the club." My blood pressure goes up. I remind her that it is Lent and that we normally do not hold baptisms until the Great Vigil of Easter. She is not persuaded and allows that "nobody" likes that long Vigil "you do at Easter." Finally, I delivered the hard news. I tell her that I follow the parish customary which was approved by the vestry. In that customary under "Guidelines for Holy Baptism," it is clear: we do not baptize during Lent, unless it is an emergency. The mother replied, "Well, you never know. Our dear thing might die unexpectedly. That would be horrible and she would not be baptized." At that point I realized that it would be a waste of her time and a danger to my health to mention a theology of Holy Baptism or to refer to the *Book of Common Prayer.* This was clearly a cultural baptism for this family, and there was not much interest in the spiritual dimensions of the sacrament. The mother left unhappy, and I never baptized that baby. Having a parish customary can sometimes give you the backbone you need in a difficult pastoral moment.

The request for a baptism on Martha's Vineyard came from a vestrywoman—not a fringe person wanting to use the church for a cultural moment, or what some have called a "Tiffany Moment." Unlike the family wanting a baptism in Lent, this family was kind, generous, and committed to the parish's ministry and mission. Was this a glorified private baptism? Do I open the door for more home baptisms, if I do this one? If I do the baptism, how will it be seen in the home parish? What is the privilege and peril of being chaplain to the rich? It often helps to list the questions you have as you face a decision in ministry.

I resented her offhand "won't Linda, of course, come with you?" The couple knew that Linda had her own parish and only four Sundays of vacation. A private plane ride...so tempting and always nice!

Yet I decided to do this baptism—for reasons I cannot totally explain. Why would I do this baptism and not the Lenten one? Was it all about the season of the church year? There is a lot of gray area in ministry. I called the grandparents to discuss the details and my terms. First, I shared my ambiguity about home baptisms, and I shared my anxiety about the perception that the rich get special pastoral care. I acknowledged my preference—that the baptism of the baby should be a parish celebration, not a family event—but I confessed that pastoral care must always find room for flexibility.

I told them I would fly commercially, and that Linda and Ellen would not be with me. I walked them through the service and requested that the service of Holy Baptism and Holy Eucharist be on Sunday morning, and not on the porch but in the living room. I asked them to help me with readers, intercessors, and other liturgical leaders. I told them I would deliver a homily. Finally, I told them that on Saturday afternoon there would be instruction about baptism for them, the parents, and godparents. Quickly, the grandfather said, "But we have a family golf event already planned for most of Saturday." I said, "Tough shit. No instruction, no baptism."

It is a good priestly habit to baptize as part of a public service, as set forth in the rubrics of the *Book of Common Prayer*. Private baptisms send all the wrong messages. Yet, there are times when pastoral sensitivity might trump best liturgical practices. After hearing the story of the twenty-eight year old who wanted to be a Christian, I knew that it would be cruel to insist upon a public baptism. I arranged for a private service the day before the scheduled baptism. Two of his friends witnessed his "new birth." It was a holy moment, and I feel I did the right thing. A new Christian with trauma in his past is not the only time pastoral sensitivity is required. Always, the sacraments and the pastoral offices intersect with people's lives and stories. The sacraments and the pastoral offices do not stand in isolation; rather, they shape the community's life and give deeper meaning to the individual lives.

"Any baptized person may administer Baptism." So states the rubric in the *Book of Common Prayer* in the section of the Additional Directions entitled "Emergency Baptism." The service is simple: water is poured as the baptizer says, "I baptize you in the Name of the Father, and of the Son, and of the Holy Spirit." The Lord's Prayer follows and other prayers, if so desired. I arrived at the hospital to administer emergency baptism. I baptized the newborn and said the Lord's Prayer. We were all crying, full of questions and scared about what the future held for this vulnerable soul, this beloved child "marked as Christ's own forever." Because of my schedule that day, I was not wearing a clergy shirt. I did not have priest's stole. I did not have a *Book of Common Prayer*. None of that mattered. What mattered was the sacrament, pure and without ceremony.

Instructions for the parents and godparents are very important. When the family walked out at the Peace after having their baby baptized, I said to the congregation: "I hope no one else leaves. Please come forward and take some of the best seats in the house." The family's premature exit really bothered me. I surmised and put the worst interpretation on the event: baptism for these folks was a cultural or personal family moment.

It was not about the family of God. It was not a sacramental moment. The luncheon at the country club following the service was more important than Holy Eucharist.

The family who left before Communion taught me an important priestly habit to practice when coming to the waters of baptism: Remember at the class for baptismal instruction to attend to both theological *and* practical matters. Reminding those who are part of the baptismal party to stay until the dismissal is a good idea! Keep in mind that non-Episcopalians will be clueless about the service, if you do not take the time to explain it. You will be utilizing a vocabulary which could be like a foreign language. Do not assume the non-Episcopalians will know what a font is. Will they recognize a ewer? The theology of baptism is not simple. Take some time to clarify the life and death significance of this initiatory Christian sacrament.

Other priestly habits I have found important over my years of priesthood have to do with the practical aspects of the sacrament, like what to wear and what to say. If Holy Baptism is set in the context of the Holy Eucharist, wear an alb and white stole. (If it is the Feast of Pentecost, though, then wear red. Priests do not get many chances to wear red stoles.) If Holy Baptism is a service without Holy Eucharist, cassock and surplice are acceptable. An emergency baptism is just that—what you are wearing is unimportant. It does help to have some of the Prayer Book committed to memory, since you may be called to do an emergency baptism without much preparation, and there are parts of the baptismal service in which you may need to concentrate on holding a baby rather than finding your place in the Prayer Book.

Remember that the *Book of Common Prayer* identifies four major feasts for Holy Baptism, but you should be pastorally flexible. In some parishes, Holy Baptism is scheduled once a month. The size of the parish and the number who are likely to be baptized in a given year dictate planning and require flex-ibility.

Be bold as you pour the water from the ewer. Touch the water when you bless it and make the sign of the cross. Do not be penurious with the water. It has become my custom to as-perge water over the congregation as I offer the Peace, follow-ing the actual baptism. The children closest to the font enjoy this moment, and it invites the people in the congregation to renew their own baptismal vows. Having towels nearby for the baptism and the aspersions is important.

It is often at the Peace that the newly-baptized is given a gift, such as an embroidered baptismal towel, certificate, or candle. A lighted candle can be dangerous with an active baby nearby. Be vigilant.

Respect crying babies. Do not assume that you know how to hold a baby. Be aware: active babies grab microphones, stoles, noses, eyeglasses, and ears.

Should you ever decline to baptize? While scheduling must be considered, I have never declined to baptize an infant—al-though, as with the story of the visiting family who wanted a private christening and had already reserved the club, there have been times when family expectations made the baptism impossible for me to do. I have never baptized a young person or adult unless I was confident that their decision was thought-ful and informed.

Baptism is serious business—but do not spend your life cor-recting people who talk about "christenings" instead of "bap-tisms." Whatever word you use, you are being marked as Christ's own forever. Your life will be different. Your bap-tismal/christening day becomes as important as your birthday. You become part of a larger family, the family of God. Certifi-cates are given to mark the occasion—signed by the baptizer. Prepare and sign these before the day of the baptism, so they are not forgotten or carelessly done. Baptisms (regardless of their location—hospital, private home, nave) should be recorded in the parish registry. You may be invited to a lunch-eon afterwards, so you will need to think about whether to go or not. What do you do if there is more than one luncheon? I took each occasion of Holy Baptism as its own with its own peculiar circumstances. I found it was best not to be rigid about these things. I think the priest should take part in festive events that celebrate sacramental moments, being part of the congregation as it lives life on many levels.

One more habit before we move on: Keep your note cards handy. When you are asked at coffee hour after a baptism, "If a person is not baptized, will he/she go straight to hell?" If you quickly say "No," then you may hear: "Well, then why bother?" Good question. What do you say? It might be well to point out (here is where a bit of theology comes in handy) that as part of the human family, we are all God's children from birth. Baptism does not *make* us God's child; it is not an insurance policy to keep us out of hell. Baptism gives us a distinguishing mark: the sign of the cross. Baptism gives us our Christian name and identity. We enter the church, the body of Christ, through the waters of baptism. Holy Baptism welcomes us into God's family, the church. The presider and people say to all who have been baptized: "We receive you into the household of God. Confess the faith of Christ crucified, proclaim his resurrection, and share with us in his eternal priesthood." Holy Baptism promises new life to God's beloved child. In the assurance of faith, the church prays for the newly baptized, immediately after they receive the water.

The craft of priesthood must get right the two primary sacraments, baptism and Holy Eucharist. The other holy sacraments are surely part of living that craft which is shaped by water, bread, and wine. And so we turn to the celebration of the Holy Eucharist now.

Chapter 3

Keeping the Feast

The altar is where all the "spokes" of my ministry connect. When I was ordained a priest in 1980, it was a time of much conversation about the meaning of the Holy Eucharist, the place of the Holy Eucharist in the life of the church, and the frequency of its celebration. The 1980s saw the Episcopal Church living into the 1979 *Book of Common Prayer,* which emphasized the prominence of the Eucharist as the normative Christian liturgy when the assembly gathers on Sunday. After decades of arriving on Sunday morning for a principal service of Morning Prayer, Episcopalians were learning that the Christian liturgy on Sundays should be a celebration of the Eucharist. Daily Morning Prayer was just that: an office with prayers and readings for daily use, but not for corporate Sunday worship. In my first parish as an ordained leader, the Eucharist was offered (was it really celebrated?) once a month. On other Sundays, people were happy with Morning Prayer and a sermon. Too much Eucharist was seen by many as not a good thing.

By the time I went to the Church of the Ascension in 1981, there had been a gradual movement toward more frequent celebrations, but I rather quickly instituted celebrations on the first and third Sundays. I remember a priest in the Diocese of Western North Carolina concluding that having Morning Prayer on a Sunday morning was like getting dressed up with no place to go! There was a changing mind in the church and an emerging consensus about celebrating the Holy Eucharist as the principal service each Sunday, though it was not an easy transition for many. By the time I left Ascension in the winter of 1995, it was customary to have celebrations of the Eucharist every Sunday.

As the Episcopal Church shifted to more frequent celebrations of the Eucharist, congregations had to pay attention to the ways church architecture could be altered to enhance eucharistic celebrations. Altars were pulled from the walls of many parishes as part of theological education being offered about the Holy Eucharist, which encouraged the practice of the priest facing the congregation during the Eucharistic Prayer. No longer did the priest face the wall as the words of institution were said. If the altar was immovable, then free-standing altars or tables were brought into sanctuaries and chancels. While many churches found renewal and revitalization in these changes, they were not gladly embraced by all the faithful.

In the Church of the Ascension, the altar was pulled from the wall as renovations were undertaken to install a new Flentrop tracker-action organ. Most people were enthusiastic about the new organ. Many people were less convinced about the new placement of the altar. Once the renovations were completed, my parents came to Hickory to hear the organ and to see the changes to the sanctuary. My mother encountered one great matriarch of the parish who told her, "Well, your son has ruined our beautiful little church. We do not buy his so-called theological arguments for the placement of the altar." My mother did not help my cause, for she responded (I was told): "Oh, I don't think moving the altar had anything to do with theology. His hair is getting thin and I think he did not want the congregation looking at a shiny spot." Not what I needed, to say the least.

Theology did in fact have everything to do with the placement of the altar. As the priest faced the congregation, the people of God gathered around an altar to keep the feast. The whole church is the minister, and the gathered assembly is a priestly people led by one called to preside. Priesthood was being re-thought, just as a new sacramental theology was emerging in the Episcopal Church with the 1979 *Book of Common Prayer,* which had profound implications for the craft of priesthood.

Vignettes of the Eucharist

Keeping the feast is a solemn and joyous occasion. I am standing at the altar waiting for the bread and the wine to be brought up from the back, but the bread has arrived at the altar from the bakery in its plastic bag twisted tight. Removing the plastic twist and the bag is not the most dignified of things to do as the whole congregation looks on. How do I get the future Jesus out of the bag?

As a Lay Pastoral Assistant at St. Philip's Church in the late 1970s, part of my responsibilities include serving the bread at Communion. One Sunday I am perplexed when one well-heeled lady kneels at the altar rail and opens her hands to reveal an enormous jewel. To my surprise, it was her custom (as I later discovered) to turn her very large emerald-cut diamond around on her finger for Communion—so that the presider is blinded and forced to place the host on the exquisite piece of jewelry.

Big hats on women are not friendly props when serving the Holy Feast. On one occasion, again at St. Philip's, I come to a woman at the altar rail with her large pink wide-brimmed bonnet virtually obscuring all of her being. So, I take the bread and thrust my hand under her hat, hoping to find her hands. To her horror and mine, I drop the host into her open blouse.

When I began my ordained ministry, most readings of the burial office or funerals included the presence of the body in a casket. By 1985 in my parish in Hickory, we had a memorial garden since more and more people were opting for cremation and burial in the church garden. The Holy Eucharist with the burial office was still rather uncommon, but on one such occasion I am given a very odd request. The widow asks me to please tuck a wafer in the urn with the ashes. "I want Joe to have Communion one last time," she tells me. "We cannot leave him out."

In Baltimore I prepared a Christian woman and a Hindu man for marriage. We carefully walked through the challenges and joys of an interfaith marriage. When it came time to plan the actual service, the bride-to-be requested that the marriage be placed in the context of a celebration of the Holy Eucharist. I looked at the groom-to-be and asked his thoughts. He said: "No problem. My family and I will receive, if that's all right. We will do this out of respect for my bride and her family."

Good priestly habits,
with theological reflections

How do you discreetly take a large loaf of bread from a plastic bag that is tightly twisted? There you are: standing before God and God's people. At one level, it is no big deal. Remove the bread and without pretense fold the bag and give it to the acolyte. If there is no acolyte, place the bag under the missal stand or pillow—or somewhere. Whatever you do, do it quickly. If this happens in the parish you are serving, it might be well to have some instruction for the altar guild.

As presider, you will occasionally encounter strange behavior from the faithful as they receive the bread and wine. I had one long-term member who insisted on serving himself: he wanted to take the wafer from the paten. In general, such "quirkiness" should not be tolerated, especially when it is based on a mis-understanding of theological or liturgical principles or creates a distraction for others who are receiving the bread or wine. Individual instruction was the best choice in the case of the self-serve parishioner, as I gently attempted to explain the distinc-tion between "receiving" and "taking" this means of grace. After serving the bread a number of times to the woman with the big diamond, I mustered the courage to ask her for an ex-planation. She smiled and said: "My grandmother and mother had this custom. I never asked them why they turned their en-gagement rings in as they received. I do it to remember them. That's all. Do you think it strange?" I was honest and said it *was* strange, but that after hearing her reason, her practice made all the sense in the world. She was not showing off her jewels—as I got to know her I realized this would have been the very last thing she would have done! There was no deep theological reason for her action. For her it was a custom and a way to remember her loved ones. If we can hear people's sto-ries, we will often understand their actions. I loved serving that grand lady Communion thereafter—and thoroughly enjoyed placing Jesus squarely on the six-carat, emerald-cut Harry Win-ston diamond.

Serving women who wear big hats will never be easy duty. I did learn to hold the wafer in front of them—or to tap them on the shoulder to make "contact" if the hands are totally in-visible. If you place the wafer in the wrong place—as in a lady's blouse—do not tarry. Move on. Do not get into a conversation or apologize. Just provide another wafer. For sure, you must not attempt to retrieve the wafer. The least said is the best said, and in this case the least done is the best done! After the service, it is fine to seek out the big-bonnet communicant to offer an apology. It is well to remember that it is not a sin to be embarrassed.

In the 1979 *Book of Common Prayer*, the rubrics for The Burial of the Dead presume the celebration of the Holy Eucharist, and we are told what to do if there is no Communion. Steadily, I have seen Episcopalians embrace the Holy Eucharist with the burial office. I never imagined, however, that a person would request that a wafer be placed with the ashes in the urn.

I took seriously the widow's request. First I told her I would like a little time to think about her idea. Later the same day, I asked to see her. We talked about her loss and her husband's last days. We talked about the family who was gathering and the toll of grief. We talked more about the service we had planned. I then said that I wanted to talk a little about her request that a wafer be placed with Joe's ashes. I understood that indeed for her it would be a loving act. I then added that Communion is a foretaste of the heavenly banquet. When we eat the bread and drink the wine, we are remembering and partaking in the Body and Blood of Jesus. Jesus had such a meal with his disciples before his own death. Every time we have Communion we glimpse the kingdom, we taste and see Jesus and the future we will have with God forever. I concluded: Joe is with God forever. He cannot receive a foretaste of the heavenly banquet. He is already at the great Welcome Table with Jesus. So, we should not place a wafer in his ashes. He is having better food. With tears streaming down her face, Joe's widow got it. She said, "Yes, I know he is gone but it is not easy. I will never come to Communion again without thinking of him and my children."

The people we serve bring deep thoughts and often a deeper faith. We must take them seriously. It takes time to explain why we will not place a consecrated wafer in the urn. But Joe's widow deserved a conversation and not a quick answer.

Interfaith marriages are increasingly common. Requests for interfaith celebrations of the Holy Eucharist are a bit rare, if not problematic. There is a rich debate about "Open Communion," in which the bread and wine are given to all present, including the unbaptized. Should the sacrament be open to all, or is the Holy Eucharist a meal that can only be shared by the baptized? Clergy, vestries, and churches have spent a lot of time "word-smithing" the language of invitation that often goes in bulletins. How do we truly welcome visitors to a service in which Communion is offered? What about the seeker, who might encounter Christ through receiving the bread and wine of the Eucharist? What about the person who is thinking about the faith, but is not yet ready for baptism? These are not easy questions, and there is not one mind in the church. Clearly, there is not one mind in the church about who should receive the bread and wine of the Holy Eucharist. Most parish priests do not see themselves "safe-guarding" the elements of the Holy Eucharist—or providing them only to the baptized. Most priests simply serve all who come to the rail. Our theology presumes baptism precedes reception of the Holy Eucharist and most parishes state this fact in their church bulletins. In practice, if they do not explicitly offer "Open Communion," most parishes function with an "Open Rail."

I asked the Christian bride and the Hindu groom if we might discuss Communion as a single topic in one of the sessions in the wedding preparations. They agreed. I asked the bride why Communion was important to her. She actually made a good case. I told the groom that I understood that for him receiving was about respecting the bride and her family. This made perfect sense. I then asked each of them to tell me in less than two hundred words what they believed about God and Jesus. Well-educated and thoughtful, they spoke briefly and with clarity. I talked about the meaning of the Holy Eucharist, the death and resurrection of Jesus, and the church as the body of Christ.

As we each heard each other, it became clear that a celebration of the Holy Eucharist cannot be an interfaith event. The Holy Eucharist is uniquely a Christian celebration and has meaning for people who have a relationship with Jesus Christ as their Lord and Savior. As I talked with the Hindu groom, I recounted that Holy Baptism is the initiatory sacrament of the church when we are marked as "Christ's own forever." Baptism gives us our identity as Christians, as Communion provides our ongoing nourishment. Can you have one without the other? Perhaps, but that is a discussion for another day. The couple decided not to have Communion at their wedding.

In each of these vignettes, the craft of priesthood requires a definite patience and certain willingness to have conversation about faith matters and liturgical practices. The Anglican branch of Christendom seeks to be generous, open, thoughtful, and tolerant. Denise Levertov wrote a poem in the middle of the twentieth century which is deeply indebted to the prevailing ethos of Anglicanism. It is called "A Cure of Souls." The poem asserts:

The pastor
of grief and dreams

guides his flock towards
the next field

with all his care.
He has heard

the bell tolling
but the sheep

are hungry and need
the grass, today and

every day. Beautiful
his patience, his long

shadow, the rippling
sound of the flock moving

along the valley.[11]

Good priestly habits must be centered in patience and toler-
ance, conversation and relationships. The priest can never be
far from the "flock" which is "hungry and need[s] the grass,
today and every day." What are some other good priestly
habits when making Eucharist or keeping the feast?

Let's focus for a moment on priestly attire at the altar. Common practice is a crisp and clean alb or cassock alb. Not many
priests wear cassock and surplice for Communion. The latter
are reserved for officiating at morning and evening prayer or
at weddings and funerals when there is no Communion. Liturgical stoles cannot be thrown on at the last minute. Look at
yourself in a mirror. Be sure the stole hangs evenly and that the
orphreys match up.

What about chasubles? Some parishes have full eucharistic
sets. Other parishes assume that the priests bring their own garments. Remember that priesthood is about context. What does
the "flock" anticipate? If you want to wear a chasuble and it
is not the parish's practice, please do some education. Prepare
the flock and exercise some "beautiful" patience.

What about hand actions and other gestures? Whatever
manual actions you employ, be prepared to explain them to the
"flock." Keep your actions simple and possess a liturgical theology which informs them. Less is more. Speak clearly but
without pretense.

Keeping the feast as presider is the priest's most important
work. Prepare for a service. Wear a collar when you preside. If
there is a bulletin, look it over. If others are serving with you,

---

11. Denise Levertov, "A Cure of Souls," in *Poems 1960–1967* (New York:
New Directions Publishing, 1964), 92. Used by permission.

take the time to instruct them. Do not miss the drama of the feast. Handle the holy bread and wine with care. Never rush the service—but preside in a timely way. Remember that the Holy Eucharist is a celebration. It is a joyful meal. It is a meal of mystery and grace. Let words and actions speak loudly. A priest stands before God's people as a representative, as a vicar. Take that vocation seriously and humbly. Live the craft of priesthood carefully as you preside at the altar before the people of God.

Chapter 4

Confirming the Faith

This chapter will look at two Prayer Book services: Confirmation with forms for Reception and for the Reaffirmation of Baptismal Vows, and the often overlooked service that follows it, A Form of Commitment to Christian Service. As I write about confirmation, I am indebted to the "Habit of Priesthood" class at Virginia Seminary in the spring semester of 2011. One of my students, Jenny Replogle, did an excellent presentation as part of the team which led the class on the day that the topic was "Dealing with Teenagers and Young People: Confirmation and Adulthood." Jenny referred to an Advent sermon she preached. She spoke of Zechariah, who "has lived a full life, is secure in his standing as a priest, and has even made it to the climax of his career by entering the holy place to offer sacrifice. He is accustomed to his station in life, and his identity is fully formed." (Of course, pastorally we know that no one is ever "fully formed" and without questions about faith and identity.) Mary is in a different place, Jenny went on to say; she "is an adolescent." Physically, she is now considered a woman—she has been betrothed to Joseph—yet she has "not quite entered her role in society as a woman." Those were helpful descriptions of Zechariah and Mary. Congregations are made up largely of Zechariahs—those "affected by what has already been" and Marys—those "perplexed by the future," regardless of their chronological age. Both Zechariahs and Marys can teach us a lot about life.

I had never thought of Mary as an adolescent. As Jenny gave her report about "Current Trends, Expressions, and Needs of Young People," I realized why confirmation classes and confirmation are so very important. There has always been much confusion about the liturgy. Some see it as a very important rite of passage for teenagers and young people. But a number of parents have also said to me that we must confirm them before they leave the church. Now that's an optimistic conclusion about the young! Such thoughts make confirmation more of an exit strategy than an important part of Christian development.

In the rubrics "Concerning the Service" of confirmation, the Prayer Book says:

> In the course of their Christian development, those baptized at an early age are expected, when they are ready and have been duly prepared, to make a mature public affirmation of their faith and commitment to the responsibilities of their Baptism and to receive the laying on of hands by the bishop.[12]

Those baptized as adults are also expected to be confirmed or received.

Confirmation is about owning the faith that is within us. The laying on of hands by the bishop recalls the person's baptism, whether at an "early age" or as an adult. If baptized as an infant, the person being confirmed says "YES" to the words that were said on his or her behalf. Confirmation is about coming to a more mature faith as a Christian.

But are teenagers ready for this serious business? That's the challenge. Parents want to get confirmation "done." As a priest preparing young people for confirmation, I have often thrown up my hands in despair. The confirmation class becomes another task, along with soccer, music lessons, and homework.

12. *The Book of Common Prayer* (1979), 412.

Confirmation itself becomes another test, like taking the SATs. You need to get it done and do it well. But what does it mean?

In most Episcopal parishes, confirmation is connected in some way to the youth ministry program. Again, Jenny was clear about the value of this connection. It is vital to have "three or more adults engaged in the youth's life of faith; three or more months of service as a Christian practice; and meaningful involvement in the life of the congregation." All too often, I have seen young people attend a Sunday afternoon confirmation class as their only involvement with the congregation. Perhaps a worthwhile goal would be to have the young people being confirmed intentionally involved in the parish's worship and mission. Perhaps preparation for confirmation could involve service on the worship committee, the missions committee, and other key parish committees. If adolescence is "the human condition on steroids," then we must find a way to support and encourage such an incredibly charged stage of life. Everything is writ large and matters.

Jenny Replogle illustrated quite convincingly the passion that is adolescence. She told the class that of the fifteen September 11 hijackers who wreaked such havoc on American society, fourteen were under thirty years of age. The "ringleader" was thirty-three—and ten were twenty-five and under. Confirmation in the Episcopal Church may be about finding a way to help our young people to practice youthful passion in a better and more creative way. In *Practicing Passion,* Kenda Creasy Dean says it well:

> The Passion of Christ is good news to adolescents, not because Jesus suffers, but because Jesus *loves* them with such wild, passionate hope that even death on a cross cannot stop his determination to win them. Adolescents do not want to suffer, but they do desperately want to love something *worthy* of suffering, and to be so loved. The Christian story both authenticates adolescent passion and turns it inside out, redeeming, redirecting, and redefining it with a more profound Passion still: the suffering love of Jesus

Christ. As a result, youthful passion serves the church both as a sign of the *imago dei,* and as an energy source of enormous potential. By acknowledging the Passion of Christ, adolescent passions give way to faith; and, fueled by the energy of fierce love, this faith inevitably leads to ministry.[13]

This powerful insight holds the reason confirmation is important and must be given great attention by the church and her priests: Confirmation is an affirmation of the kind of passionate faith that "inevitably leads to ministry." It may be a cultural rite of passage for many. The passion that is "redeeming" may not be at the top of the list for some young people seeking confirmation and the parents who insist that they do it at a certain age. But let us be clear: what we do at confirmation may well lead to a ministry "fueled by the energy of fierce love." When we see confirmation or reception not as another "graduation" for young people, but rather as occasions to celebrate "youthful passion," we will find these rites do indeed "serve the church" now and for the future.

Adults who seek confirmation may not have the same "youthful passion" as the young, but they should be well instructed and well prepared for the bishop's laying on of hands. Indeed, adults who decide to prepare for confirmation are often very passionate about their faith. In a year-long adult formation course I taught for those seeking confirmation, I first allowed six to eight weeks for a serious consideration of the Christian story (scripture and tradition). Then we spent time telling our own stories, as more mature people of faith, and the final part of the course was identifying gifts and talents for ministry. So, like confirmation for young people or adolescents, confirmation for adults is about encouraging the faith which "inevitably leads to ministry."

For Marys and Zechariahs, renewing baptismal vows and "practicing passion" are necessary moments of preparation for ministry. This sense of a call to serve others is the reason we reaffirm our baptismal vows at every baptism and at the Easter

---

13. Kenda Creasy Dean, *Practicing Passion: Youth and the Quest for a Passionate Church* (Grand Rapids, Mich.: Eerdmans, 2004), 2.

Vigil—thereby celebrating over time the "good work" the Holy Spirit has begun in us. At every service of baptism or confirmation we are given the opportunity to reaffirm our vows, and remember our call to serve others. The craft of priesthood involves a lot of teaching, and preparing people well for the moments of confirmation, reception, and reaffirmation is at the top of the list. It has always been a privilege as a presenting priest to say the names for the bishop as people prepare for the laying on of hands in confirmation, or the extended hands of welcome to those who are already members of the one holy catholic and apostolic church), or the blessing of those reaffirming their "passion" for the faith.

There are times when a sense of calling to a specific ministry within the church needs to be witnessed and affirmed, using the Prayer Book's Form of Commitment to Christian Service. The form is for those who wish to "make or renew a commitment to the service of Christ in the world." If done in the context of the Holy Eucharist, the Prayer Book suggests that this "Act of Commitment" take place before the Offertory.[14] This form allows us to honor the ministry of all the baptized, and can be adapted for groups as they prepare for mission endeavors, for new vestry members as they commence their service, and for a host of other times when faithful people are committing to a new ministry, a new challenge—or responding to a new "passion."

Vignettes of confirmation

At the beginning of a twelve-week confirmation class in Hickory, I ask each young person to sign a "covenant" that they will attend each of the Sunday afternoon sessions. We talk about commitment, preparation, and the importance of confirmation. One young woman misses three classes in a row. I call her to remind her of the covenant and her responsibility to the class and to me. Her mother returns the

---

14. *The Book of Common Prayer* (1979), 420.

call to say that I am unreasonable and that she has called the senior warden.

A middle-aged adult in Baltimore attends the year-long Pilgrims in Christ program. The week before the bishop's visit, he tells me that he is not sure that he has been baptized. His parents were dead and he was raised in a small non-denominational church which no longer exists. Finding a parish registry would be virtually impossible. He says: "I don't guess this is a big deal—should I do anything?"

I plan a commitment service for new vestry members. A new vestry member calls me to express some reservations about "the service of Christ in the world." She tells me that she was never baptized or confirmed. She confesses that she is not sure that she is a Christian. She said: "I love this parish. It is my family and it is at the center of my life. I take Communion, and I care deeply about so much of what we do. I will confess, however, that I do not say the words of the Nicene Creed."

Good priestly habits,
with theological reflections

The mother called me and the senior warden to complain about my being "unreasonable." The senior warden said, "Oh, give them a break. You know they are big pledgers." I found myself between a rock and a hard place, to put it mildly!

I asked to see the young would-be confirmand with her parents. They agreed. It was a tense meeting. I showed them the covenant with their daughter's signature. I tried to make the case for responsibility and for following through with things that are important. The parents offered the good and legitimate reasons for her absences. The parents were actually to blame for not returning home in time for the classes! Can you blame the young woman? They asked if there was any way to make this right. I told them that I would be willing to offer a "make-up" three-hour session on a Saturday morning—but that all three of them must attend. Reluctantly, they agreed to the compromise.

I got donuts and made coffee. I prepared handouts for each of them. It was a good session—and we all came to the day of the young woman's confirmation with a sense of accomplishment under less-than-ideal circumstances.

I set up a time to meet with the man who was uncertain about his baptism. He had tried to find out. I told him that the Prayer Book had a provision for people just like him, in its provision for "Conditional Baptism." The rubric is clear:

> If there is reasonable doubt that a person has been baptized with water, "In the Name of the Father, and of the Son, and of the Holy Spirit" (which are the essential parts of Baptism), the person is baptized in the usual manner, but this form of words is used: "If you are not already baptized, *N.*, I baptize you in the Name of the Father, and of the Son, and of the Holy Spirit."[15]

He said: "Okay, please baptize me."

We arranged for a baptism the next day—and his family and friends gathered with us to "mark him as Christ's own forever" and to make ready for the bishop's visit in three days. I did not see this as a "private" baptism because a small congregation gathered. With the pending visit of the bishop, I was dealing with a sense of urgency which seemed to justify a quickly arranged baptism.

---

15. *The Book of Common Prayer* (1979), 313.

Now a vestry member who is not a Christian is not your every-day problem! I was totally baffled. How did she get on the slate if she was not on the rolls of the parish, one of the baptized and confirmed? In this parish it was the custom to have "associate members"—people who never transferred in but who, by faithful practice, participated fully in the life of the parish. She was a giver of record. She never missed church. She was really a seeker—and totally honest.

We set a time to meet. I told her she was practicing "Open Communion"—partaking without baptism. I told her that I, too, have difficulty with every line of the Nicene Creed, but that I say it because it is what the church believes and it is what I hope to believe completely before all is said and done. She asked what she should do. I realized that she was not ready for baptism—nor was she ready to be part of a commitment service. But she was an excellent vestry member. She was an inquirer, a seeker. She did and does take words very seriously. I told her to be gentle with herself. I advised her to miss conveniently the commitment service. I told her that the altar was the Lord's, not mine or the Episcopal Church's.

Basically, I set forth for a "don't ask, don't tell" policy. I told her to change nothing she was doing. Did that mean that I embrace "Open Communion"? Not really. I responded to a particular situation which I thought deserved pastoral sensitivity and wisdom. Did she ever get baptized? I left the parish within a year, so I will never know. I know she is faithful and caring—and that she lives like the Christian she may be becoming.

Dealing with young people reminds me of the need to think about other good priestly habits. What should young people call you? If the custom of the parish is to refer to the priest as Father or Mother, then all is well. Reverend is a bit formal and not very "Episcopal." Pastor seems not quite right. Mr. or Mrs. or Ms is too formal, it seems. The Christian name does not quite seem right. It is worth deciding what you want to be called by the young people you serve. You can be too familiar. What connotes proper respect? What name suggests an intimacy that may be inappropriate? This is all quite tricky, but it is important to get it right, realizing that boundaries do matter. Think through your preferences—and make the issue a topic of conversation with children, youth, and parents.

If a young person tells you a secret, what should you do? What training do you need to be a counselor to young people? Remember there is a difference between treating something as confidential and keeping secrets. One is respectful, but the latter leads to nothing good. Each priest should be conversant with civil as well as canon law. Working with young people cannot be treated lightly. Post-seminary training is always required. Most dioceses now have training courses about professional boundaries. This should not be a course taken once. Refreshers are important. Also, lay leaders are required to take the same training—arrangements should be made for parish training or for full participation in a training event offered by the diocese.

Should you report abuse to social services or to law enforcement? Yes. You must understand the laws of the state in which you serve. You must protect yourself, even as you protect those you serve.

How do you use your office? Should you meet with a young person alone in your office with the door closed? Do the office doors have windows? Should you meet with a young person—or anyone for that matter—if no one is in the building except you? Most clergy work in solo ministries and with little or no staff support. It is difficult to take necessary precautions or to be sensitive about even perceptions. This is not a gray area. Be clear about the professional protocols you will follow and publish them in a parish publication.

Young people are precious and vulnerable. Their very "passion" requires the priest to be vigilant about words and actions.

Words can damage easily and actions can be misunderstood. Wrong messages can easily be sent. Signals can easily get crossed.

Ministering to young people may be one of the hardest parts of the craft of priesthood. It is serious business. Be clear, open, and honest with the young people you serve as priests. Keep their parents and other concerned adults in the loop. Now more than ever, ministry with the young is *shared* ministry. I have come to the conclusion that specialized ministry to young people is ill-advised unless the priest has been trained. Ministering to young people depends on knowledge of other disciplines, such as psychology and sociology. Most priests are not equipped to do such ministry well, and this is a problem area for most parishes since because of limited resources, parishes are not often able to have a "trained" youth worker.

Priests wear many habits as they offer their craft. No one is gifted in all areas of ministry, and limitations must be acknowledged. Develop relationships with the children and youth of your parish so as to be as fully their priest as their parents'. However, do not consider carefully engaging in specific, intensive work with young people unless you are qualified, trained, and mindful of the complexity of this ministry.

Chapter 5

The Celebration and Blessing of a Marriage

Of all the sacraments, I think it is the Celebration and Blessing of a Marriage about which I have the most ambiguity in living the craft of priesthood. The cultural notions of a wedding often obscure the sacramental significance of this liturgy in the Prayer Book. So much time, focus, and energy go into the wedding day that the church's blessing is almost an afterthought and the marriage itself somewhat of a footnote. It becomes a celebration about a single day, not about a life. I cannot count the times that I have heard someone say, "Well, we have gotten the club, so I want the church on such and such a day."

Some of my ambiguity derives from the divorce rate in the United States today, when some fifty percent of those "whom God has joined together" will not stay together. Standing before a bride and groom and offering the church's blessings, I often find myself wondering: will this one last? This is certainly not the most edifying thought.

I have seen small fortunes spent on weddings. I have seen a family spend as much on the flowers for a wedding as the parish church would spend on outreach for a whole year. I have been pushed to the raw edge of sanity by more than one mother of the bride. Early in my ministry, I stopped meeting alone with the mother of the bride. This was a wise decision.

There are, however, other not-so-superficial reasons which leave me ambiguous about marriage. Marriage is a mystery. Why do two people come to the church for a blessing? We sometimes talk about the "solemnization" of a marriage. Why do people submit to such sacred solemnity? As a priest officiating, I have often thought of myself as an intruder in some sacred, mystical rite. The couple who marry each other before family and friends are the ministers here, or the protagonists in a drama like that which Jesus attended at a wedding in Cana of Galilee. The priest plays a small part as he or she offers the church's blessing. Why does that blessing mean so much? In the church we talk about marriage as a lifelong process not a singular event, a life not a day. In both the Old and New Testaments we discover the roots for the sacramentality of marriage: the institution of marriage embodies or expresses God's love for God's humanity. Marital imagery is often used to describe Christ's relationship with the church, offering one sacramental, mystical act as a metaphor for other sacramental, mystical relationships.

Since the Council of Trent in 1546, marriage has been understood by most in Christendom as a sacramental rite—even as our understanding of the rite and of marriage itself has changed dramatically. There is in marriage an inward and spiritual grace—even as there are those outward and visible signs which can sometime confuse and torment us on the so-called wedding day. Jeremy Taylor, chaplain to Charles I, spoke of marriage as a "labor of love" in a sermon on "The Marriage Ring; or, the Mysteriousness and Duties of Marriage," noting that it has within it the "delicacies of friendship, the blessing of society, and the union of hands and hearts." Indeed, Taylor alludes to what it is often claimed: marriage is about order in society.

John Keble spoke of marriage as a "holy token," thus referring to the spiritual dimension of a union which is about sexual consummation and "mystical union." More recently, the Most Reverend Rowan Williams, the Archbishop of Canterbury, in a sermon entitled "Unveiled Faces," concludes: "Marriage presents us, more clearly than any other human relationship, the unity of truth and love, clarity and charity. That is one of the many reasons for the fact that it has been found so rich a metaphor to describe the relation of God and humanity."[16] This insight from Archbishop Williams points to the complexity that a priest encounters: marriage is truly personal but it is also sacramental. It reveals our humanity, even as it reveals the God who created us.

The Book of Common Prayer declares that Christian marriage is a "solemn and public covenant between a man and a woman in the presence of God."[17] The Catechism says that marriage or "holy matrimony" is a "life-long union" with "vows before God and the Church."[18] In the 1928 *Book of Common Prayer,* marriage was about procreation, order in society, and the joy of human love. The 1979 *Book of Common Prayer* reordered the significance of marriage: the joy of human love is the first reason ("the union of husband and wife in heart, body, and mind is intended by God for their mutual joy"); then the social dimension ("for the help and comfort given one another in prosperity and adversity"); and finally procreation ("when it is God's will, for the procreation of children and their nurture in the knowledge and love of the Lord").[19] This rethinking of marriage should make it easier for the denomination to accept same-sex blessings and Christian marriage between people of the same sex—but such is not yet fully the case.

Marriage is very much about this material world, our bodies as well as our souls. The church speaks easily about the spiritual dimensions of marriage. Quietly, the embodiment of marriage goes unattended. In her provocative poem "Face to

16. Rowan Williams, *A Ray of Darkness: Sermons and Reflections* (Cambridge, Mass.: Cowley Publications, 1995), 200.

17. *The Book of Common Prayer* (1979), 422.

18. *The Book of Common Prayer* (1979), 861.

19. *The Book of Common Prayer* (1979), 423.

Face," Denise Levertov writes about an intimate relationship, possibly a marriage:

> We plunge—
> O dark river!
> towards each other—
> into that element—
>
> a deep fall,
> the eyes closing as if forever,
> the air ripping, the waters
> cleaving and closing upon us.
>
> Heavy we are, our flesh
> of stone and velvet goes down,
> goes down.[20]

The emotional, sexual, material reality of marriage is not something the *Book of Common Prayer* helps us with. In another poem, Levertov offers additional thoughts "About Marriage." In this poem I find articulated the complexity of human love and the challenge of marriage—and the very reasons it is a sacrament not easily administered. Levertov confesses:

> Don't lock me in wedlock; I want
> marriage, an
> encounter—
>
> I told you about the
> green light of
> May....
>
> It's not
> irrelevant:
> I would be
> met

20. Denise Levertov, "Face to Face," in *Poems 1960–1967* (New York: New Directions Publishing, 1964), 164. Used by permission.

and meet you
so,
in a green

airy space, not
locked in.[21]

Leave it to the poet to express that which is inexpressible. What is human love? What is sexual love? What is a union which is about mutual joy? What is divine love? How do marriage vows capture the mystery of human love? It is no wonder that I have often arrived at the wedding day filled with ambiguity. What exactly am I presiding over?

Clement of Alexandria encouraged his flock to take "advantage of marriage for help in the whole of life, and for the best self-restraint." Finally, this may be the worst case for marriage and best explanation for my concern as officiant at the Celebration and Blessing of a Marriage. As a priest I have often felt that I was simply an agent of the state to insure domestic tranquility and the whole of corporate life. Marriage, after all, enhances the social order of human life. But the priest who is thinking must also ask, what makes a marriage Christian? Of late, with the discussion about same-sex blessings and marriages, it is more than ever necessary to understand marriage and what the church is doing in its blessings. Of course, it is not easy to understand a mystery. I think Levertov makes a lot of sense. Marriage is an "encounter," a place where we are not "locked in," a place where we "plunge—O dark river!" Marriage is a "deep fall" and the church offers her blessing to such mystery, to such a natural longing between human beings.

Vignettes of marriage

It is one of the first weddings at which I am to officiate at Trinity Church in Asheville, and I arrive at the rehearsal unprepared for a ceremonial innovation. Without ever men-

---

21. Denise Levertov, "About Marriage," in *Poems 1960–1967* (New York: New Directions, 1961), 140–141. Used by permission.

tioning it, the young couple has decided to include in the wedding party a miniature bride and groom, dressed as the actual ministers. I am appalled.

A bride comes to me with two ceremonial requests: a long white runner down the center aisle on which she and she alone would walk, and the unity candle. With respect to the latter innovation, she asks that one candle be lit from two candles and that only the single candle for "unity" would remain lit.

I have been asked to officiate at a big, society wedding. I learned of this big wedding from the mother of the groom. Now, usually it is the mother of the bride who is to be feared, but the groom's mother comes to my office to protest the wedding. She says, "Everyone knows that my son has been living with this girl for several years. She may be pregnant. I think you should tell them to go to the court house and save us any embarrassment." I tell her to ask the young couple to come to church and to meet with me afterwards so we can find a time mutually acceptable to discuss their pending nuptials.

The young couple is charming. I know both of them slightly, and they tell me that yes, they have been living together, but their deep commitment to each other seems real and inspiring. They know about all the family conversations behind their backs. The young woman says, "I want a big wedding and I want to wear a white dress. I am not pregnant. All my friends wore white dresses—and they all have slept around more than I have." Well, this is more than I want to hear.

After a number of counseling sessions and after meeting with the parents of the bride and the groom, I allow a conventional wedding—but do draw the line about the secular music they have chosen for the entrance procession: "Here Comes the Bride" (or the "Wedding March" or "Bridal Chorus") is from the 1859 opera *Lohengrin* by Richard Wagner; I insist upon sacred music instead.

The day of the wedding comes. The mother of the groom is wearing an original suit of silver threads by Carolina Herrara. It is appropriate armor. All of the family's tensions and all of my anxiety erupt at the point in the service when the officiant is to ask, "Who presents this woman to be married to this man?" In a bumbling moment, before several hundred of the city's most prosperous, I say, "Who presents this *mother* to be married to this man?" The fears of the families become a truly awkward liturgical *faux pas*. I look immediately to my wife, Linda, who is sitting on the fourth row of the gospel side of the nave. She smiles and gives me a thumbs-up, even as I imagine the moving vans in front of our house.

Good *priestly habits, with theological reflections*

Miniature brides and grooms are a no-no! While it might seem to the real bride and groom to be a fun way to include children in the procession, it is actually a benign form of child abuse. Furthermore, it is tacky! While I was appalled the first time I witnessed the practice, I did not forbid it. But I learned that it is important to have a parish handbook or customary for the Celebration and Blessing of a Marriage which protects the parish and priest from such ceremonial innovations. While some see the wedding day as an elaborate production, the priest must work hard to keep the focus on the sacramental meaning and purpose of Holy Matrimony.

White runners are an old-fashioned ceremonial innovation which should be forbidden in the parish customary for weddings. Some liturgists leave open the possibility of unity candles; again, if you have a customary for marriages, you can be specific at the beginning of the negotiations about the wedding. Under no circumstances, though, should you find yourself agreeing with the bride who wants only one candle left lit. Blowing out two candles to signify unity is just plain stupid. If marriage is an "encounter" (as Denise Levertov holds out hope for), then two unique children of God are part of the mystery. The Prayer Book, in one of the optional concluding prayers, asks God's blessing on the *two* people in the marriage, not one: "Send therefore your blessing upon these your servants, that they may so love, honor, and cherish each other in faithfulness and patience, in wisdom and true godliness, that their home may be a haven of blessing and peace." Nowhere in the order of service does it say that the couple will become "one flesh." In unity we remain ourselves and thereby there is the potential gift of "encounter," of mystical union. So, if there must be unity candles, leave all three candles lit.

At the Peace of the wedding of my big *faux pas* about "who gives this mother," I apologized to the couple for ruining the service. They both said it was an honest mistake—forget it. I approached the mother of the groom (fearful for my very life), who responded that we would need to talk. The father of the bride asked if I knew something he didn't.

The next week I visited the family. We talked about the tensions that accompanied the day and my subconscious anxieties as I navigated the rough waters of the family dynamics. We talked about the culture of the small town we loved, about our greatest fears and hopes for those we love and live with. We reflected theologically, and I asked them about God's place in all the wedding plans. The wise father of the groom said, "You know, I don't think we remembered to invite God." In the end, a big thing became a small good thing.

This wedding forced me to rethink the parts of the parish's customary which addressed the Celebration and Blessing of a Marriage. In consultation with my Worship Advisory Committee and the vestry, I resolved that going forward both members of the couple would be presented: "Who presents this man and this woman?" My big *faux pas* left me with other resolutions. It is important to make notes before presiding or officiating. Prepare carefully a presider's or officiant's edition of the service. Take seriously the rehearsal. Don't forget to take a moment before the service for that last-minute look. And above all, forgive yourself quickly.

There are other good priestly habits to keep in mind when it comes to weddings. Prepare the ministers (the couple) well for the service. Take seriously the marriage counseling—usually three sessions at least. It may be wise to outsource the majority of the counseling to pastoral therapists in your area. We cannot have all the skills necessary for ministry. Good pre-marriage counseling requires training, time, and expertise.

Up front, I assert that marriage is a sacrament—not a Hollywood occasion. I find it helpful to wear a black cassock at the rehearsal and to begin with a prayer. Celebrations and blessings of marriages should be first and always services of worship. To help make this clear, I always request a crucifer (part of the acolyte core or a person trained especially for the occasion), making sure that the congregation stands because the cross has entered the space, not because the bride is coming down the aisle. Having the crucifer is one way to address the inevitable "liturgy of the wedding dress" syndrome. Behind the crucifer should be the liturgical party and then the wedding party, including the groom and best man. No one should slip in by a side door, like a thief in the night. The crucifer should also lead the recessional. Do not allow visible photographers during the service. Discourage, if you can, the applause which sometimes erupts as the bride and groom exchange their first kiss. Of course, discouraging applause is virtually impossible, but you can be clear about the parish's custom during the rehearsal.

The rubrics in the *Book of Common Prayer* in the service for a marriage leave as optional the preaching of a homily "or other response to the Readings." It has been my custom to preach a homily. This is probably part of my evangelical heritage peering out from my chasuble. These days, many people never go to church unless they are attending a wedding or a funeral. As the priest presiding (if a Eucharist) or officiating (if there is no Eucharist), you should not miss the opportunity to proclaim the gospel, to tell the good news of Jesus Christ. The "Readings" should be passages from scripture—but you might well allow other readings, such as poems, as responses to the scriptural selections provided in the Prayer Book. Never let people write their own vows. Remember: it is the church's service, not the couple's. The vows or prayers a couple may write at twenty-five years of age are not what they will write when fifty or sixty and may not reflect the breadth of the commitment being made. The words in the Celebration and Blessing of a Marriage in the *Book of Common Prayer* are elegant and timeless.

At the end of the service, do you do the stole-binding? Some say you should avoid this ceremonial custom because it draws too much attention to the priest. It is, however, a powerful symbolic action to emphasize that "those whom God has joined together let no one put asunder." The priest represents the church and conveys God's blessing. It seems right to bind the right hands of the couple with the stole: an outward and visible sign of that inward and spiritual grace, that "encounter" which is mystical.

Finally, let me offer a few words about liturgical dress and the party afterwards. If there is a celebration of the Holy Eucharist following the Peace, the presider should wear an alb

with a white stole. If it is the parish's custom, wear a chasuble.
If the service concludes with the Peace (where the bride and
groom often kiss), the officiant should wear a cassock and surplice with white stole. A cope may also be worn—otherwise,
as one of my students observed, "you're in your underwear!"

Parties go with weddings. Often the clergy are invited. If it
is a formal wedding, remember that a clergy collar with a dark
suit is just fine for a man or a woman. Polished black shoes
will take you a long way! As you attend the wedding party, you
are still a representative of the church. You are the one who
conveyed God's blessing. It is your sacred role. Do not step out
of your "habit." If asked to provide a blessing over the event
or the food, be gracious. Yes, we know that all people can
pray—but asking you may well be a way of honoring you. Put
the best face on the request. If alcohol is served and if you partake, then do so with some restraints in mind. Wearing the collar to a party should keep you mindful and respectful of your
craft.

Chapter 6

Reconciliation and Ministration to the Sick

So far in this book, we have discussed being a priest at the baptismal font and at the altar. Living the craft of priesthood also includes the work of the "pastoral offices" as they are detailed in the *Book of Common Prayer*. We have already considered Confirmation, A Form of Commitment to Christian Service, and the Celebration and Blessing of Marriage. Now let us consider other pastoral offices: Reconciliation of a Penitent, and Ministration to the Sick. The last pastoral office is the Burial of the Dead, and is the concern of the next chapter.

In the order of service for The Reconciliation of a Penitent, after the penitent's confession to having sinned "by my own fault in thought, word, and deed, in things done and left undone," there follows a rubric: "Here the Priest may offer counsel, direction, and comfort."[22] Flippantly, I have often said that confession is good for the soul. Too right! In the Episcopal Church confession is most often a corporate act in the context of the liturgy on Sunday, but in some parishes priests hear private confessions on a regular basis. In other parishes, Lent be-

---

22. *The Book of Common Prayer* (1979), 447.

comes the season of individual confessions as the faithful prepare for Easter Day.

Confession is hard work—whether done by an individual
or a group of sinners. It is about remembering our sins—
"things done and left undone." So, once a priest has heard a
person's confession, what should be "the counsel, direction,
and comfort" offered? My counseling has often included wisdom from *The Golden Grove*, written by Jeremy Taylor in
1655. In a section entitled "Agenda; or, Things to Be Done,"
the great Anglican Divine says:

> Receive the blessed sacrament as often as you can. . . . Con-
> fess your sins often, hear the word of God, make religion
> the business of your life, your study, and chiefest care; and
> be sure that in all things a spiritual guide take you by the
> hand.[23]

Unpacking this ancient wisdom makes the words seem very
modern. After hearing a confession, what else could you say
before you say the absolution that would be more pertinent
than Taylor's counsel: Remember to "receive the blessed sacrament"; keep confessing your sins as you hear God's word;
make your religion or faith central to your daily life, study, and
"care"; and take a "spiritual guide" by the hand. Today we
would say to take a "spiritual director" by the hand. Either
way, this is sound advice for the seventeenth century and for
the twenty-first!

The absolution is given after words of counsel. God's word
of forgiveness is conveyed by God's priest to the individual penitent. If confession is hard work, giving absolution is holy
work. In the sixteenth century, Thomas Becon, chaplain to
Archbishop Thomas Cranmer, grounded absolution in the writings of the prophet Malachi when he wrote in his *Potation for
Lent,* "The prophet Malachy saith: 'The lips of a priest keep
knowledge; and men shall seek the law at his mouth: for he is

---

23. Jeremy Taylor, *The Golden Grove, or, A Manual of Daily Prayers and
Litanies,* in *The Whole Works of Jeremy Taylor,* vol. 15, ed. Reginal Heber
(London: C. and J. Rivington, 1828), 40.

a messenger of the Lord of hosts.'"[24] At the absolution, the priest is a "messenger of the Lord of hosts." In a real sense, the priest does not learn this craft. It is a divine gift. It is awesome: the priest speaks for God. If there were ever any doubt, the moment of absolution makes it clear: priests are different. Their craft is not every Christian's craft. By virtue of ordination, priests are given power to bless and to absolve. Never is a confession heard without an absolution given.

Becon was also concerned long ago about what the penitent would hear in the absolution. He instructed penitents:

> And when he shall rehearse unto you the most sweet and comfortable words of absolution, give earnest faith unto them, being undoubtedly persuaded that your sins at that time be assuredly forgiven you, as though God himself had spoken them, and according to this saying of Christ, "He that heareth you heareth me:" again, "Whose sins ye forgive are forgiven them." This have I spoken concerning auricular confession.[25]

None of us hears forgiveness easily, just as most of us find it difficult to forgive ourselves. But it is deep within the thought of Anglicanism that if the penitent hears the priest, the penitent hears Christ himself. Priests are vicars of Christ.

What is true for individual confession is also true for corporate confession. While, sadly, many priests never hear individual confessions, all priests hear corporate confession or many confessions at once—and then give a corporate absolution with the sign of the cross over the faithful who are penitent.

I suppose it would be better if all counseling done by priests were in the context of the rite of the Reconciliation of a Penitent. Counseling undertaken by priests ought to have a spiritual dimension, since the counseling is actually part of the congregation's care and ministry through the priest. And the *Book of Common Prayer* sets the counseling within liturgy, the place

---

24. Thomas Becon, *A Potation for Lent*, in *The Early Works of Thomas Becon*, ed. John Ayre (Cambridge: Parker Society, 1843), 101.
25. Becon, *A Potation for Lent*, 102.

where Anglicans and Episcopalians "do" their theology. Of course, this is often not the case. Priests are often more counselors than confessors. In some ways this confuses the craft of priesthood and can even add to the woes of the priests. When counseling is done outside of a liturgical rite, such as the one for Reconciliation, the message is not always clear. Is the counseling spiritual or psychological? The craft of priesthood is multifaceted, and the role of the priest as confessor is very important. Likewise, the role of the priest as absolver is holy and right. The priest as counselor can quickly become a complicated terrain to negotiate.

Closely tied to the rite for the Reconciliation of a Penitent is the rite of Ministration to the Sick. If the priest is God's "messenger" in confession and absolution, it is clear that in ministering to the sick the priest is "pastor" and the healer is Jesus Christ. Prayers and the laying on of hands are all done in the name of Jesus and for the sake of Jesus.

Bishop John A. T. Robinson, whose bestselling book *Honest to God* ignited a theological fire storm, was concerned about sickness and healing after his cancer diagnosis in 1983. Robinson concluded that health means wholeness—and is concerned not "simply with cure but with healing the whole person in all his or her relationships." Priests minister to those who are sick in body, mind, spirit, and relationships. The wholeness of sickness suggests the wholeness of health. Robinson was interested in "faith-healing." Robinson has been most helpful to me in his assertion that healing is not about pessimism or optimism; it is not about "good days and bad days, remissions and recurrences." Rather, the Christian "takes his stand not on optimism but on hope."[26] Robinson then appeals to Paul, who teaches us that God is our hope because of the resurrection hope that is the other side of the grave for Christians. Robinson believed that Paul in his mind and writings "had risen with Christ" long before he died.

Perhaps that says it all. As priest, we must encourage those who are sick to endure, to live with Christ, to have hope—now

---

26. Eric James, *A Life of Bishop John A. T. Robinson: Scholar, Pastor, Prophet* (London: Fount, 1989), 309.

and even beyond the grave. Healing services are more and more part of Episcopal parish life. These are times to teach and to preach about that which Robinson writes so eloquently. Healing is about wholeness not a cure. Sickness is not about judgment or sin. The laying on of hands (with anointing) is as holy as the moment of absolution. For over a decade at Ascension in Hickory and during most of my five years in Baltimore, the most gratifying part of my parish ministry were the services in which I joined the people of God in praying for health and for wholeness—and often against the greatest of odds. The craft of my priesthood was at its best when I would lay hands on the faithful and say: "I lay my hands upon you in the Name of the Father, and of the Son, and of the Holy Spirit, beseeching our Lord Jesus Christ to sustain you with his presence, to drive away all sickness of body and spirit, and to give you that victory of life and peace which will enable you to serve him both now and evermore. Amen."[27]

Vignettes of confession, counseling, and healing

A solid, hard-working man asks to see me about something weighing heavily on his mind. We meet in my office. He tells me about the last days of his wife's illness with tears streaming down his face. He begins to tell me about administering morphine to her in the last weeks of her life. Suddenly, I stop him from talking and say, "Let's move over to the sanctuary. Let me hear your story as a confession." I think I am suggesting such a sudden shift in location because I see where he is going. We go over to the church. He kneels and I put a chair beside the rail in the sanctuary. I hear him tell me how he increased the morphine and hastened his wife's death. "Did I murder her?"

---

27. *The Book of Common Prayer* (1979), 456.

A very attractive woman in her mid-thirties who is a member of the parish asks to see me in my office. She arrives and, as she is walking into my office, my assistant tells me that the woman's sister-in-law is on the phone and wants to talk to me as quickly as possible. I tell my assistant that I will call her after the appointment. My assistant looks at me and pronounces, "Not a good idea." My communicant tells me that she is facing some difficult issues and wants me to be her counselor. She is dressed in a provocative short skirt and is wearing very high heels—not exactly the best way to dress on a Thursday morning at 9 a.m. to see the rector. After about forty minutes of conversation in which she tells me some rather embarrassing and distressing things, she suddenly stands up and abruptly leaves. As she walks out of my office after what I thought was a truncated and somewhat odd counseling session, she says in a loud voice, "That was very inappropriate." My assistant follows me into my office and says, "This is serious. Her sister-in-law was trying to get to you before you saw her. She has said that she was going to charge you with sexual misconduct."

A dear man on the search committee that presented my name to the vestry at the Church of the Redeemer is diagnosed with a lethal cancer within my first six months as rector. He calls to tell me the alarming news, a man in his prime, full of life and committed in countless ways to making the world a better place. Immediately, I go to Butch's home to be with him, Sally, and their wonderful daughters. He asks, "If you got this kind of news, what would you do?" Without missing a beat, I say I would go to a healing service to pray for myself, for the doctors, and for all who love me. I would pray for healing and hope that would mean a cure. I would not give up. I would fight the cancer like hell and I would pray with all my being. So, Butch replies, "Well, let's have a healing service." I look at the calendar, set a date, and begin planning for a Sunday night healing service the following week. I do not notify the vestry, and get word that some vestry members are concerned about a healing service. One man calls me and says, "Redeemer is not into snake-handling and magic. What are you doing?"

Good priestly habits,
with theological reflections

Hearing a confession about a man overdosing his wife with morphine was not an easy day's work. I listened to this suffering soul with every ounce of my being. He increased the morphine as he saw his wife's pain from bone cancer become more and more unbearable. Did he hasten her death? We will never know. Was he trying to end her life? I concluded no; he was trying to end her pain. Did he have anything to gain from her death? Not really. Did he murder her as he thought? No, he did not kill her. His actions were driven by love and compassion. I told him all these things. I then took his hands in mine and said, "In a moment I will lay hands on your head. I will anoint you. I will call your name and say a prayer. In God's holy name, I will grant you absolution and God will forgive you. You must hear the words and believe what your confession and my absolution have to say about your wholeness, about the healing of all your memories. You loved your wife and cared for her as you thought best at the time. Let go of the last weeks, her pain and your agony. Remember the love you shared and accept God's love and forgiveness." This was hard work. It was holy work and I felt the presence of God.

When I heard the words "sexual misconduct," I knew I was in deep water. I called the bishop, the senior warden, and then an attorney. I wish I had listened to my assistant—but that is water over the dam. Suffice it to say, this was a painful time in my ministry. Not many people knew about the anxiety which was mine for a number of months. I wondered if I would ever do any more counseling. It is a treacherous territory, and the priest may never be more vulnerable than when trying to be helpful as a counselor. Words can be twisted and actions misunderstood. Is it worth it? I lived through these false charges but came out on the other side rather chastened. Every season of ministry has "dark guests," and occasionally they come in the guise of parishioners. Following the practices and procedures of Safe Church training and your diocese can protect the priest as well as innocent parishioners.

Healing services can be misunderstood. I acted too quickly at the Church of the Redeemer. I should have enlisted the support of the wardens and vestry—and even my staff. I stepped out in front of everyone because I was trying to respond to Butch's request. Despite these missteps we had the service in the parish's chapel. The place was packed. I asked the man who wondered about "snake-handling" and whether or not this was a "Redeemer kind of service" to come. The service was well publicized, and for almost eight days I did nothing but prepare people for the parish's first healing service. On the Sunday morning before the afternoon healing service I preached about healing, being cured, and the mystery of God's wholeness. To this day, the Church of the Redeemer has a Sunday afternoon healing service. It became part of the parish's ministry and, I think, part of the parish's wholeness.

Here are some other good priestly habits to develop in offering pastoral care. I think it is important to hear individual confession before the altar in the sanctuary and chancel. If there is an altar rail, use it. As priest-confessor, you can sit in a chair on the altar side of the rail. For a long time I did not use holy oil for anointing; I simply laid hands on the person desiring healing and absolution. I now see how both oil and hands laid convey the deep truth of reconciliation and ministration of the sick. You see, these two pastoral offices overlap in countless ways.

Serving Communion to the sick is another way to minister to the sick and to offer prayers for wholeness. Don't assume that everyone wants Communion. It pays to ask—just as it is wise to ask about the laying on of hands with anointing.

In homes and by the sides of hospital beds, priests are called to be of courage and of hope. As confessor, absolver, and healer in Jesus' holy name, priests do work that only they are given to do. Individuals and the faith communities in which they live are never fully well. There is sickness in us all and in every faith community. Confession and prayers for healing are the ongoing work of the faithful.

The work of reconciliation and ministration to the sick are at the very core of the craft of priesthood. If the priest does these things well and with heart, the congregations they serve will believe what is proclaimed from the pulpit and understand more fully what is done at the altar.

Chapter 7

The Burial of the Dead

I f I come to services of the Celebration and Blessing of a Marriage with ambiguity and even dread, I approach the task of presiding or officiating at the service for the Burial of the Dead with a strange peace and joy. I do not think I have ever conducted a service using the order for the Burial of the Dead without hearing expressions of gratitude from family and friends. Some say (and I would agree) that the liturgy for the Burial of the Dead is the *Book of Common Prayer* at its very best. It has always been a privilege to begin a service with the powerful statement of faith: "I am the resurrection and the life, saith the Lord; he that believeth in me, though he were dead, yet shall he live; and whosoever liveth and believeth in me shall never die."[28]

In W. H. Auden's poem "The Age of Anxiety," the character Malin has a thought:

> We're quite in the dark: we do not
> Know the connection between
> The clock we are bound to obey
> And the miracle we must not despair of. . . . [29]

---

28. *The Book of Common Prayer* (1979), 469.
29. W. H. Auden, "The Age of Anxiety," in *Collected Longer Poems* (New York: Random House, 1934), 350.

No family comes to the church for the funeral of a loved one without some sense of darkness, some sadness, some despair. Even when death is expected, "we're quite in the dark." Yes, we know that we are mortal ("the clock we are bound to obey"), but we yearn to connect our dying to the "miracle we must not despair of." That miracle is proclaimed in the opening anthem of the order of the Burial of the Dead in the *Book of Common Prayer:* "For none of us liveth to himself, and no man dieth to himself. For if we live, we live unto the Lord; and if we die, we die unto the Lord. Whether we live, therefore, or die, we are the Lord's."[30] That same great claim is often restated when we hear in the service the conclusion of the iconic reading from Romans 8:

> For I am convinced that neither death, nor life, nor angels, nor rulers, nor things present, nor things to come, nor powers, nor height, nor depth, nor anything else in all creation, will be able to separate us from the love of God in Christ Jesus our Lord. (Romans 8:38–39)

Such faith assertions are not easy to hear sometimes. In the months following my ordination as a deacon, I found myself comforting a family who had lost a son and his wife in a tragic traffic accident. Upon hearing the horrible news, I went to the house with no words to say. I think mine was a ministry of presence that day. A day or two later, I returned to the house. As the front door opened, I saw two closed caskets sitting in the great hallway. It was more than one could stand. Those caskets held people snatched from a full life in their early thirties. How could the world be so "dark"? Where was there a connection to the "miracle we must not despair of"?

In Hickory I presided at the funeral of a baby who died at four months of age. I got through the service by pure grit. At the graveside, after most of the mourners had departed, I stood helpless and overcome with emotion. Yes, I knew that "we are the Lord's," but in a brief moment I questioned it all. How could it be that a loving God would allow such a sadness, such

---

30. *The Book of Common Prayer* (1979), 469.

a loss? Is there a God after all? Living one's priesthood is never without doubts and the loneliness of the dark.

During one Holy Week, I got the call that a twenty-year-old parishioner had committed suicide. The custom in that parish was that the burial service was usually two or three days after the death. As the family thought about the service, they asked if it could be held the morning of Good Friday. The funeral home already had funerals scheduled for Saturday. Without missing a beat, I said that of course we could have a service of resurrection hope on Good Friday. After the Maundy Thursday stripping of the altar in the evening, the altar guild reentered the empty sanctuary, vested the altar in stunning white, arranged glorious flowers, and prepared for the reading of the burial office and celebration of the Holy Eucharist. Immediately after the 10 a.m. service, the nave was returned its bare starkness for the noon Good Friday liturgy. I realized that even Good Friday could not keep the church silent in the face of death. "O death, where is thy sting?"

Vignettes of meeting death and sorrow

I am preparing for a burial office at Trinity Church, Asheville when I receive a request from a friend of the family: please allow all the flower arrangements to be at the chancel steps and in front of the pulpit and lectern. I am told that this is the parish's "custom" at funerals. The lady making the request then tells me that her sister would be sending a very special arrangement which would include a blue princess telephone. The ribbon on the bouquet would have the words: "Jesus calls us."

In Baltimore, a young woman has died of cancer. She came to Redeemer during her illness because of some of her friends. Her family was uninterested in the church. I am with the woman when she dies, and I administer the last rites, surrounded by grieving family members who have no faith to sustain them in this trying hour. Moments after her death, her sister asks me about the service. Can we please have an open casket?

A long-time but inactive member of the parish has died. I knew her, but not very well. Pastoral care for her in her last years had been provided by other clergy and Stephen Ministers. The family asks that I "do" her funeral and that I offer a eulogy. I agree, knowing that I would offer a homily of resurrection faith with some references to the faithful departed. Another priest on staff plans the service and meets with the family while I am out of town. The day before the service I return late and weary from travel.

The service for the Burial of the Dead was to include a celebration of the Holy Eucharist and committal afterwards in the parish's columbarium. Just before the service, I quickly look over the bulletin. My homily is handwritten and unfinished.

I step into the pulpit to face a nave full of mourners, and begin delivering my homily, giving thanks for a life well-lived. I make some general comments about the faithful departed, even as I pull myself into a meditation on our resurrection faith. Suddenly, my eyes land on the face of an elderly woman sitting close to the front of the chapel. I am horrified. I thought she was the deceased, the person I was burying. She is very much alive, thank you very much! I was remembering the wrong person. I think I turned purple. In the twinkling of an eye, my vestments are wet with perspiration. I am truly petrified, and think I am going to explode.

Miraculously, I finish the homily—making a few strategic changes. I wonder: did anyone notice? The service concludes and we process to the columbarium with the congregation. As people enter the parish hall for a reception, I place myself at the door—as was my custom—to

greet the congregation. The dear dowager whom I was trying to bury comes up to me in full sail. She says, "Dear Barney, that was such a divine service! For a moment I thought
you were talking about me." I lie and say, "No way!!"

Good priestly habits,
with theological reflections

Once again, it is helpful to have a parish customary that ad-
dresses the ways in which the particular parish conducts the
service for the Burial of the Dead. Having numerous floral
arrangements should be avoided. Be clear: altar flowers and
possibly flowers to adorn the paschal candle are sufficient.
There can be a spray of flowers on the casket or urn—but not
in the church. In most parishes, the altar flowers are arranged
by the altar or flower guild. There is no reason to bring in mul-
tiple arrangements from other suppliers. There is a certain
democracy about a funeral in the Episcopal Church. Whether
prince or pauper, the same words are said. The pall over the
casket or urn insures equality for the faithful departed. Some
people might have a hundred floral arrangements from family,
friends, and associates. Others might have none.

Most Episcopalians would quickly say "no open casket" under
any circumstances. In the particular situation here, I listened
carefully to the family's wishes. I heard the typical arguments.
Some people did not get to see her near the end of her life. Others are used to open caskets and will need such for closure at
the time of this death. The woman was so young, suffered so
long, and was part of a family and a culture that always had
open coffins or caskets. The more I heard their concerns, the
more I was inclined to honor their request. So, I suggested an
open casket at the funeral home but not at the church. As it
turned out, the family could not bear the cost involved in having what is called a "visitation" at the funeral home. Finally, I

proposed that the "visitation" or wake could be the night before the service. The body could lie in state with the casket open
in front of the altar. On the day of the service, the casket would
be closed and covered with the white damask pall. The family
was grateful for my flexibility—and it all seemed right for that
particular family. Even when you have a parish handbook that
sets forth clear policy, you must accept that "one size does not
fit all" and that exceptions are the norm. The craft of priesthood can never be some rigid adherence to a set of guidelines.
Pastoral grace must be informed by but not limited to a set of
guidelines in a parish handbook or customary.

Burying the wrong person should be avoided at all cost! I never
mentioned my error for as long as I was at that parish. I was
truly mortified. How could I be so stupid? So careless? Now,
over ten years later, I tell the story with great embarrassment.
If at all possible, know well the person for whom you are offering the burial office. This may not be always possible, especially in a large parish or if you are new to the congregation. If
there is a parish pictorial directory, do consult it. If at all possible, meet with the family of the faithful departed and be part
of the service planning. Ask the family and loved ones about
stories that they would like for you to share—which does not
mean you must share them all. Remember that eulogies are inappropriate; the *Book of Common Prayer* says a homily "may
be preached," and the homily should be a proclamation of our
resurrection faith—not a biographical recitation. At the same
time, the homily should not be generic—it should reflect the
ways in which the faithful departed lived out the church's resurrection faith.

It is well to remember other good priestly habits in caring for
the dying and bereaved. Be articulate about your own theology

of death, resurrection, and eternal life—but remember that it is a work in progress. People ask thoughtful questions when they face death head-on. Do not give careless answers. When possible, be with a family at the time of death. The Prayer Book provides a service for such a moment, Ministration at the Time of Death.[31] Visit with the family of the faithful departed—preferably in their home, but definitely at the church as well. Carefully plan the service with family and friends. This is therapeutic and can be part of dealing with the loss and grief. Remember the complexity of family systems. If the deceased is a member of your parish, do you have on file their final wishes? When scheduling a service, the primary consideration is the availability of the church. While priests should guard their days off, pastoral care at the time of a death trumps a priest's schedule. As an old priest once told me, people die at such inconvenient times. If there is a casket, what considerations must you make? Who takes the casket down the aisle and how? Does the family follow the casket or enter earlier or by a side door? Each parish has its customs—be sensitive to the prevailing culture. As with a marriage service, having a crucifer is advised.

The Book of Common Prayer presumes a celebration of the Holy Eucharist, with the Burial of the Dead as the Liturgy of the Word. As with all services, follow the rubrics of the Prayer Book. They are there as directions, not as suggestions!

At the Commendation, the clergy should draw near to the casket or urn, which should be where the paschal candle is also located—or as the Prayer Book says, "The Celebrant and other ministers take their places at the body." The current Prayer Book makes no allowance for ashes instead of the body. If the body is not present in some form, there is no commendation and the service concludes with the blessing and dismissal.

Committals take place at the grave site. On occasion, families request a committal before the reading of the service for the Burial of the Dead. Most often, the committal follows the Commendation, either at the church or at a nearby cemetery. Remember to insist upon real dirt for the Committal, not the

---

31. *The Book of Common Prayer* (1979), 462–467.

sanitized sand in a small plastic container that is often provided by funeral homes and the like. If possible, pull back all of the artificial turf and get a handful of the real thing. There is something holy about making the sign of the cross with the dirt on the casket or urn, acknowledging one last time that the faithful departed was, is, and will always be marked as Christ's own forever.

Of course that raises the issue: do you offer a Christian burial for the person who was not a believer or who was not baptized? Sometimes it is better not to ask a host of questions. A child of God can and should be commended to God by God's church.

As with the other pastoral offices, wear a cassock and surplice if you are not celebrating the Holy Eucharist. Some priests wear a black tippet as they read the burial office. If the service for the Burial of the Dead is the Liturgy of the Word for Holy Eucharist, then wear an alb and eucharistic vestments. Most often I have remained vested for the Committal, whether at the church or at the cemetery.

If there is a reception after the service, please attend. Do not rush off to other pressing matters. People only die once. Take some time to be present with family, loved ones, and friends. Follow up a week or so after the service with a phone call or note.

As we know, grief takes its own time. It was my practice in the parish to remember the anniversary of a death with a card and a brief note. Officiating or presiding at a service for the Burial of the Dead is a great privilege. It is part of the deep and multilayered relationship between priest and people. The service and your leadership becomes part of the parish's narrative— and as priest we become part of the families with whom we find ourselves in great joy and in great sorrow. Cherish those relationships in parishes large and small. If a priest gets his/her craft right at the critical times, then many things may be forgiven in ordinary time.

Chapter 8

Administrative Stewards

In my first parish as an ordained person I attended the vestry meetings, though as curate and then associate, I was rarely on the agenda. Much of the conversation was about the budget and the allocation of resources for ministry and mission. There was more talk about ministry than mission. If I did not exactly disdain the vestry meeting, I thought that it was at best too much about business and not enough about the church. I was naïve.

In 1981 when I became a rector, I had much to learn. It was the custom at the Church of the Ascension for the rector to chair the vestry meetings. (In some churches it is the senior warden who conducts the meetings.) So, at my first vestry meeting at Ascension in October 1981, I found myself at the head of the table with very little confidence. I was suddenly chairing what I had once disdained or thought was much ado about business. There was a considerable learning curve, and I will always be grateful to the vestry members at Ascension. They were patient, instructive, respectful, and kind with their very green thirty-one-year-old rector. But learn I did.

The very year that I became a first-time rector an exciting new book appeared: *Ministry and Imagination* by Urban T. Holmes III. It was sublime reading for me. In the very introduction, Holmes said he did not have "much sympathy" for a "business as usual" response to the "crisis of ministry." For him the "crisis" was playing church—pretending that we are "still living in seventeenth-century in England or on the nineteenth-century American frontier." Holmes criticized congregations for letting "memorials accumulate" in the midst "of a great bustle of activity in the altar guild, acolyte organization, and boys' choir."[32] I had no idea he had been to my parish! Holmes reserved his strongest words for priests who have

> their portrait painted on their twentieth anniversary in one of two poses. The first pose is in a worn cassock—growing slightly green under the armpits—standing in a field of daisies with little children hanging on their cincture. It is reminiscent of nineteenth-century paintings of Jesus. The other pose is in an ornate cope, standing by the altar, with one hand clutching the *People's Anglican Missal* and the other resting on the fair linen.[33]

I knew I did not want to be the director of social programs in Hickory. I wanted to be a rector of a serving congregation—but I was not quite sure what that meant. Holmes was calling for a conversion of ministry in the Episcopal Church. I was new and none of my cassocks were "green under the armpits." Reading his thoughtful book, however, got me thinking: what am I doing when the vestry meets and what am I doing at the altar? In other words, was my craft of priesthood about the practical as well as the spiritual? Did the two have much to do with each other?

To complicate matters, I was living in a time when there was a great deal being published about priesthood. This may have been precipitated in the Episcopal Church by the continuing debate over the ordination of women. There were a number of writers who emphasized the professional identity of priests. Of course, this would be where we would locate priest as administrator and director of programs. Even priest as counselor seemed to fit in such an identity. Others were claiming that priests are linked to the symbols. This is what Holmes was working on in

---

32. Urban T. Holmes III, *Ministry and Imagination* (New York: Seabury Press, 1981), 5–6.
33. Holmes, *Ministry and Imagination*, 6.

Ministry and Imagination. Holmes insisted that a priest is a sacramental person—and he believed so in at least two ways.

First, the priest is "symbol-bearer." Paul writes in his first letter to the Corinthians that they should "think of us in this way, as servants of Christ and stewards of God's mysteries" (4:1). Holmes interprets this verse to mean that "we are 'administrators,' 'managers,' even 'treasurers' (all possible translations of *oikonomoi*) of the 'hidden things,' 'secret rites,' the 'mysteries' (the word *musteria* is what the Greek Church uses for 'sacraments') of God." For Holmes, the priest is a sacramental person because he/she is also a symbol. He writes:

> Again Paul, who actually knew nothing of the ministerial priesthood, writes: "For the same God who said, 'Out of darkness let light shine,' has caused his light to shine within us, to give light of revelation. . . . We are no better than pots of earthenware to contain this treasure, and this proves that such transcendent power does not come from us, but is God's alone" (2 Cor. 4:6–7).[34]

These were big insights for a new priest who was also a new rector. How would I be a "symbol-bearer" in a relatively low church congregation? Moreover, what would it be like to be a symbol-bearer of that which I am also? I knew that being a sacramental person was also about mystery. How does the priest help the faithful draw near to mystery, to the transcendent? How does the priest connect earth to heaven? Holmes argues that the priest "is essentially an inhabitant of the *limines* (he is a 'liminal person')"—one who stands on the threshold "*between* the structure and the antistructure."[35] Clearly, such a theology of priesthood leaves little room for "business as usual." For me, it also meant that the practical and spiritual belong together. There is no time for a change of dress, if you will. The habit of priesthood must make room for what happens in vestry and for what occurs at the altar. Both contain symbol and mystery—and the priest presides over both.

---

34. Holmes, *Ministry and Imagination*, 220.
35. Holmes, *Ministry and Imagination*, 221.

The priest does have a professional image like the lawyer, doctor, or teacher. But priests are also "servants of Christ and stewards of God's mysteries." The priest is both servant and steward. Priests serve the cause of Christ in the church and the world. They are not servants of their congregations—that would be a role doomed to tension and conflict. There has been a lot written about servant-leaders. We may be missing the point. What does it mean to be a "servant of Christ"? The vocabulary of leadership can be very helpful—and I will turn to it in a moment—but most insights into leadership do not capture the spiritual component. To be a servant of Christ suggests a priesthood that is not about us but about Christ. Being a servant of Christ implies a craft which is practical and spirit-focused. As priest—as also with the priesthood of all believers—we follow the One we serve. Servant leadership can imply a way of being "up front." Perhaps being a servant of Christ suggests something about serving—being unseen and not noticed.

Understanding the vocation of "servant of Christ" is as difficult as making sense out of the vocation "stewards of God's mysteries." Priests are stewards of the sacraments, but as "servants of Christ" they are also stewards of God's greatest mystery: God's church. This is where the practical meets the spiritual; the temporal meets the timeless; the structure meets the antistructure; and the earthly meets the heavenly. For sure, it is where ministry meets administration.

Max DePree, in his fine book *Leadership is an Art,* wrote that he was often asked, "What is your personal goal for [the furniture company] Herman Miller?" He would reply:

When one loves jazz, one thinks of Louis Armstrong. When one truly enjoys baseball, one thinks of Sandy Koufax. When one appreciates stabiles, one thinks of Alexander Calder. When we respond to the French Impressionists, we think of Renoir. Each of these beautifully talented, beautifully trained, beautifully disciplined persons is special to us because he is a gift of the spirit. My goal for Herman Miller is that when people both inside the company and outside the company look at all of us, not as a corporation but as a group of people working intimately within a covenantal relationship, they'll say, "Those folks are a gift to the spirit."[36]

Administration is holy work and very much part of the noble craft of priesthood. It encourages and makes space for the range of a parish's "gifts of the spirit" to find expression.

Vignettes of administration and daily work

Many in the congregation said that a new organ was needed. Others thought more attention should be given to the parish's outreach program, specifically that the parish should fund a major initiative being coordinated by community soup kitchen. The vestry decides to learn more about each of the needs from the parish's Worship Committee and Outreach Committee. The Worship Committee presents a series of questions: What kind of organ—for example, electro-neumatic or tracker action? Which comes first: interviewing organ builders or organizing a capital campaign—or do you do these tasks simultaneously? Would this be the work of the Worship Committee—or a new Organ Committee? Would the Organ Committee be about selecting an organ and about raising money to pay for it? And so forth.

The Outreach Committee presents a strong case for the parish's leadership in the community's outreach. They too ask a number of questions: What percentage of our budget goes to outreach and mission? Are we doing our part in the community? Are the needs greater than they used to be?

The vestry acts wisely, and in a wonderful moment of Anglican both/and rather than either/or, decide that the parish is called to do both. The vestry asks the rector and wardens to set up a new Organ Committee to research or-

---

36. Max DePree, *Leadership is an Art* (New York: Dell Publishing, 1989), 61–62.

gans and possible ways of funding a new instrument; it would report to the vestry. The Outreach Committee would be empowered to have conversations with the governing board of the city's soup kitchen about needs and funding. The vestry requests that these research projects be completed within six months.

In six months the vestry receives the reports from the Organ Committee and the Outreach Committee. Could the parish really have a new organ and spend almost an equal amount on an outreach project?

The Adult Education Committee did not complete its summer work of organizing the Sunday morning classes for the coming academic year. The rector discovered this the week before opening Sunday and the first adult education class of the season. On opening Sunday, the rector stands before the adults who are gathered and says, "Well, this morning we will plan the offerings in adult education." Immediately, a vestry member stands up and accuses the rector of "embarrassing" the Adult Education Committee before the "whole" church. "You should have planned a few Sundays to cover us," he tells the rector. "You should have known that the planning was not complete."

I am having lunch with the daughters of a rather wealthy woman. In our conversation I tell them that their mother, before her tragic death, had promised to change her will and help with a major parish project. When the parish received a copy of her will, we found that we were given $20,000. I ask them if they might consider helping with the project to honor their mother. One of the daughters asks if I am telling them that their mother intended to leave the parish more money. She is gone and there are no witnesses to that conversation. "How much would you like each of us to give?" they ask. Being on the spot and not having much time to think, I say that I would like each of them to give $100,000. They both agree, and dessert is ordered.

Good priestly habits, with theological reflections

Priests must be co-workers with the people they serve. A popular prayer of Oscar Romero, the archbishop of San Salvador who was martyred in 1980, reminds us that we are "workers, not master builders, ministers, not messiahs." Priests should not find themselves on pedestals. Think of the liturgical stole as a towel of servanthood. The priest who serves as rector must work with the vestry and other parish leaders. The rector serves on the vestry, and the vestry should not meet without the rector—unless when discussing compensation.

Being prepared goes a long way in ministry. Look ahead. Do not wait until the last minute to prepare for a sermon, a service or a meeting. As a priest, be careful to account for the gift of time. There will often seem not enough time in the day to do the work which is before you. Yet there really is enough time to accomplish the tasks which matter and which are truly at hand.

When I asked my parish members for gifts of $100,000, what was I thinking? Was it a number pulled out of thin air? To be honest, it was. I had not done my research. I quickly calculated what interest income would helpfully augment our music budget. I was not, however, prepared to make an "ask." Fund-raising is part of being an administrative steward—it is about present needs and future ministry. Ministry and money go together. Priests must find ways to talk about money and what faithful people do with their money. Money can be sacramental—and many people want very much to give for God's mission in the world. Do not neglect people's time, talent, and treasure.

A priest must become familiar with the language of estate planning, trusts, and various instruments which people can use to give for the future—and not to give now! In the *Book of Common Prayer* there is a rubric at the end of the service A Thanksgiving for the Birth or Adoption of a Child. It is sort of the last word, if you will:

> The Minister of the Congregation is directed to instruct the people, from time to time, about the duty of Christian parents to make prudent provision for the well-being of their families, and of all persons to make wills, while they are in health, arranging for the disposal of their temporal goods, not neglecting, if they are able, to leave bequests for religious and charitable uses.[37]

Administrative stewards who are priests should attend to such practical matters as wills, even as they preach from time to time about money, about how we use the money we have now and how our money might be used after we are dead.

Whether at a vestry meeting, before an adult education class, or when having lunch with a church member, be mindful of your appearance and prepare well for your presentations. There are priests who only wear collars for services or for liturgical duty. Others see the clergy collar as a sign of their sacramental ministry. Priestly ministry is always sacramental—an outward, visible sign of what God is doing in us and in God's church. So whether in collar or dressed as a professional, whether preaching or sharing conversation at coffee hour, presiding or tending to the administrative needs of the congregation, priests must remember that they are always a vicar of Christ, one who helps people connect the human to the divine.

---

37. *The Book of Common Prayer* (1979), 445.

Chapter 9

Of Registries, Customaries, and Other Necessities

ood practices are often understood as good liturgical practices. I have suggested which liturgical vestments are best, such as a simple white alb when presiding at the Holy Eucharist. If officiating at a daily office, the vestments are cassock and surplice with black tippet. Resist lace trimmed albs and surplices. Resist stoles made with felt and glue. Well-meaning parishioners will give you homemade stoles. Accept them graciously and, if necessary, wear them once. Good practices for men and women often include polished black shoes, very little jewelry, and no cologne or perfume. I keep it simple. If reading Daily Morning Prayer or Daily Evening Prayer or other offices, remember that it is not about you. Speak clearly and slowly—but do not be overly dramatic. If presiding at the Holy Eucharist, decide your style and which manual acts fit you. Do nothing at the altar which you cannot explain to the people of your parish. They will ask: why did you cross yourself at that point? You will want to be able to answer cogently.

Good practices also extend beyond the public liturgies and the pastoral offices. Priests are well served if practices are clearly stated and easily understood. The "paperwork" of priesthood—

marriage licenses, parish registry, parochial reports, vestry and committee minutes, strategic plans, parish guidelines, and customaries—cannot be treated as insignificant. They matter.

When officiating (if there is not a celebration of the Holy Eucharist) or presiding (when there is Holy Eucharist) at a Celebration and Blessing of a Marriage, the priest is both an agent of the state as well as the church. This means those who are marrying each other will go to the local court house to get a marriage license. This license must be filled out and signed by the officiating priest. When do you do this? Some priests sign the license as part of the service. Some do the "paperwork" at the rehearsal, often the night before. There are "purists" who say that the marriage license should not be signed by the priest until after the service or ceremony. Whenever the license is signed by the priest, the couple, and their witnesses, it must be returned to the authorities in the mail.

Celebrations and blessings of marriages must be recorded in the parish registry. Indeed, the parish registry should contain the record of all parish services—and any services conducted by the parish clergy off-site. The bishop on his/her annual visit to the parish often examines the parish registry. All Sunday and weekday services are recorded there, along with the names of liturgical leaders and the number of those in attendance. Baptisms and marriages are included, and each time the burial office is read. If the priest does not keep the parish registry, he/she must identify the person or persons who will manage this important "paperwork." Often, altar guilds are given the task of keeping the parish registry. Whoever keeps it, priests must still remember to sign each entry, as presider, officiant, and so forth. Such parish records are very important. They are a great resource for historians, and they can be helpful in pastoral situations as well. I have searched the parish registry to find a baptismal date for a person who did not have a birth certificate and was applying for Social Security benefits. Keep faithfully this important record.

A well-tended parish registry will help the parish priest when it comes time to complete the annual parochial report for the diocese. The parochial report includes information about all services and the parish's finances. In some parishes, completing the parochial report is the concern of the priest; in others, there is a division of duties to include those responsible for the financial records of the parish. The final compiled data of the parochial report must be verified and signed by the priest who is charge—or, to use an old-fashioned term, the priest "who holds the cure."

Vestry and committee minutes, parish guidelines, and customaries are very important "paperwork." The priest who is the rector is a member of the vestry. Vestry minutes are legal and historical documents. They should be carefully written and approved by the vestry. If the parish has committees of the vestry or committees outside the vestry, it is prudent to have a policy that all meetings result in notes which can be subsequently approved. Vestry minutes and committee notes are just good business practices. There will be parishioners who will insist that the parish is not a business. They are wrong. Yes, first, the parish is part of the larger church which is the body of Christ. But the parish is also a business, very much in this world, yet not of this world.

Many parishes have by-laws and other guidelines about vestry elections, terms of office, and other administrative matters. By-laws need to be revised from time to time. The priest should be familiar with the parish by-laws and other documents approved by the vestry. By-laws are not incidental to parish governance. Increasingly, parishes are seeing the wisdom of strategic plans, documents which identify priorities and provide timelines for parish goals. Strategic planning should be a vestry priority, and not driven by the priest or rector. A good strategic plan will help a parish priest accomplish the work which the parish has decided is important. A good strategic plan will provide focus and will be an important guide for both priest and vestry. Writing strategic plans is an art. Priests need to know when they should have expert advice. Strategic plans may be the area where an outside expert or consultant will come in handy. The process which leads to a strategic plan is as important as the actual plan. Implementation of a strategic plan can provide the framework for vestry agendas and the ministry of the parish. Having a strategic plan protects the priest and often informs in positive ways the ongoing reflection and periodic assessment of the parish's and the priest's ministry.

Parish customaries should be on the desk of every priest. Parishes are well-served by by-laws and other parish guidelines, and so it is with customaries. Customaries traditionally address the liturgical customs of the parish. If a strategic plan protects the priest when it comes to implementing the work of the parish, a well-written parish customary is like wearing a bullet-proof vest in the liturgy. A customary saves the priest from flying by the seat of his pants or inventing as she goes along. Let me provide some examples.

The customary can be clear about the parish's Sunday and weekday services. How is one trained to be a reader? The customary should be clear about the education required for acolytes, chalice bearers, intercessors, ushers, eucharistic ministers, altar guild members, and others associated with worship. What are the parish's policies about flowers for baptisms, marriages, and funerals?

In particular, the customary will be clear about Holy Baptism. Utilize and expand or adjust, if necessary, the rubrics and guidelines of the *Book of Common Prayer*. For example, some parishes find it necessary to have baptisms monthly and not only on the occasions listed in the Prayer Book. The customary is a theological primer as well as a guidebook. Holy Baptism is initiation into the community of faith and is not a private service. The customary can offer a theological case for sacraments and services.

Please remember: adverbs are important qualifiers. Customaries can never be written in stone. Customaries provide clarity for the theological and practical case made about a certain sacrament or service—but flexibility must always be the handmaiden of parish ministry. Customaries will include those customs unique to a given parish. When I was the rector of Ascension, Hickory, there was delightful custom of giving an embroidered baptismal towel to each person being baptized. This was mentioned in the parish customary.

The parish customary should include the practices around confirmation, reaffirmation, and reception. How is one prepared for baptism, confirmation, and all other sacraments? The age for confirmation in one parish may not be the age for confirmation in another. Clear guidelines will be helpful.

The parish customary can be a life-saver when preparing for the Celebration and Blessing of a Marriage. All sorts of customs have risen up around weddings. The customary can be straight-forward about what is allowed and what is forbidden, so that when a couple requests the participation of a young or "miniature" bride and groom, or brides and their mothers request a white cloth down the center aisle to keep the wedding dress pure and clean, the customary could say they are not allowed. When a family wants to spend $100,000 on flowers, the customary can have specific guidelines from the flower guild. The unity candle is a favorite request; the customary can be clear about this custom—or say that it is not allowed. The customary would ideally be clear that parish clergy officiate or preside at marriage services, and may insist upon only sacred music and note that the parish musician will assist in planning the service. If the parish charges for use of the space, the customary should set forth the fee structure. May rice be thrown at the newly married? The customary might be quite clear that those cleaning up after a service will be given additional compensation. Such detail is important and, if in the customary, the priest may be spared endless explanations. Each parish has its own customs—and new priests never have a clean slate when it comes to a parish's liturgical practices. We often inherit customs—and must adjust to living with them.

The section in the parish customary on the Celebration and Blessing of a Marriage could also contain guidelines regarding second marriages. Permission is required from the bishop for priests to officiate at second marriages. Many dioceses have policies about third marriages and more. The parish customary ought to contain such information.

At the time of death, many families find it difficult to make decisions. In the planning of a funeral, a parish customary can be a very important document. What does the service look like without a celebration of the Holy Eucharist? If the Eucharist is celebrated, what are the parish customs? Will the body of the faithful departed be present—or ashes? Or will it be a memorial service? How are these services handled? The parish customary could address the matter of remembrances by family and friends at a service. Does the parish allow eulogies? If so, when do they occur in the service? The customary should be clear about the theology which informs the burial service in the *Book of Common Prayer*. Are floral arrangements allowed in the worship space? If there is a body, is the pall optional? All of these details can and should be addressed in the parish customary.

The parish customary should always be close at hand and in a format that is easily shared with parishioners. Such customaries can even be a text for an educational series, as for example, in an adult education series about the Holy Eucharist, the Daily Offices, the sacraments, and the pastoral offices. Such classes can provide occasions for parishioners to plan their own funerals and to complete forms which contain their wishes. Teaching with the parish customary provides an opportunity for parishioners to learn more about the Bible, the *Book of Common Prayer,* the hymnal, and other musical resources. The parish customary can open up a discussion of the theology which informs the church's liturgy and the parish's worship practices.

Most parishes are not well served by having nothing beyond their oral tradition. Of course, the oral tradition, the "we have always done it this way," is part of every parish's DNA. Being attentive to the "paperwork" of a parish should be at the heart of the ministry of a parish priest. Whatever the venue, priests must be mindful of that ministry which is in the office and behind the scenes. Be mindful of the details. Good business practices are often good priestly practices.

Chapter 10

Dark Guests in the Craft of Priesthood

M ost of us struggle with the ghosts of our lives. We rarely call the ghosts by name. The bundle of complexity and ambiguity which I am is well-staffed by ghosts. Actually, I fastened a long time ago on a Puritan phase, "dark guests," which is from a prayer in *The Valley of Vision.*[38] I have entertained a number of "dark guests." The "dark guests" were not necessarily evil. They were "dark" because my relationship with them was mysterious and full of unknowing. There were a number of "dark guests" on my path to Holy Orders. Because of these "guests," I am more somber, more self-aware, and more suspicious of "Mother Church." The "dark guests" never really leave me—but the darkness seems less pronounced as the years go by. I suppose ghosts and "dark guests" become like shadows—yet are still very much a part of who I am and what I do as a priest.

The craft of priesthood is composed of much more than the visible etiquette and ethics of a professional life. Most would agree that the priest's life can be lived in a "fishbowl," where

---

38. "The Dark Guest," in Arthur G. Bennett, ed., *The Valley of Vision: A Collection of Puritan Prayers and Devotions* (Carlisle, Pa.: The Banner of Trust, 1975), 71.

all actions and decisions are carefully scrutinized. Well-meaning parishioners can become fixated on the external practices of their priest. I was so aware of the fishbowl life while serving in Hickory that I traded cars only when necessary and only when I could find a car just like the model I was driving. I did not want comments about the rector's new car. Of course, when it came for the "roast" after Evensong on my last Sunday, there was a fine skit about the rector's three gray boxy station wagons during his almost fourteen years of service-with photographs to document the rector's car-trading practices. Interest in my car-trading practices suggests a deep interest in the personal or private life of the public priest. Where I went on vacation was of interest. What I wore while cutting my grass on my day off mattered. How my wife dressed was of interest. At a party, someone was counting my trips to the bar. If one of my children hit a rough patch growing up, it was of interest to the parish. If I was under the weather, the parish wanted details. If I mentioned a book I was reading in a sermon, the local bookstore would get orders for that book. The skit revealed that there is a desire to "look into" the lives of parish priests, to read them like a book—and to search for both flaws and authenticity.

While a priest deals with living in the fishbowl of ministry, he or she must also deal with that which is hidden from view. There is coterminous with an exterior ministry of etiquette and ethics an interior life which no priest wants "read like a book." The exterior life of priestly practices is connected to and shaped by the interior journey, the journey which is not for public scrutiny. In that interior life is light and darkness, joy and pain, peace and conflict. Often, priests walk through their inner lives with therapists and spiritual directors. It is certain: one cannot be an effective priest without attending to the inner journey. Over the years, I have been more and more mindful of the darkness, pain, and conflict in my own inner journey. I am aware that my sermons often emerge from the shadows of my life, from the places which have not been photographed for a parish skit. There are dark guests who inhabit my interior life.

Unattended, these dark guests can ride into the exterior life, causing lots of trouble, pain, and conflict.

We must decide how we read the text of our inner life. Perhaps this is an important decision which each priest (or Christian!) must make. How will I read or interpret the narrative of my inner life? Naming the dark guests may be a good first step. So, let me name some of the dark guests common to priests who are reflective and thoughtful, who struggle with their own incarnation as they proclaim the Word which is made flesh.

Dark guests include our family of origin; the twins of classism and elitism; the threesome of race, gender, and ethnicity; sexuality; careerism; and the complexity of human relationships. None of us must endure all of these—but no one lives with only one dark guest. Paul wrote of his "thorn in the flesh." If dark guests are like Paul's thorn, then all of us live in a thicket of thorns. There is not in the human condition the luxury of one thorn.

Family of origin is a dark guest to be reckoned with. How we relate to others and make decisions can be connected to the ways we were shaped in our family of origin. Our relationship with our parents and our place in the birth order are but two of the important markers which have an impact on the exterior life we live as an adult. Reliving my childhood has taken a lot of my energy as an adult. As I have gone deeper into my priesthood and as I listened over and over again to the stories of my parishioners, I have also gone deeper into my own story—an exercise both difficult and critical.

Classism and elitism can be very dark guests. It is often said that education is the avenue from one class to another. The Episcopal Church of my childhood in South Carolina and early priesthood in North Carolina assumed a certain class structure. I only knew a white, upper middle-class, well-educated church. In my hometown, the Episcopal Church was home to the doctors, lawyers, business leaders, and many of the people "who had money." Such classism can easily breed a certain world view which is problematic, if not antithetical, to the gospel. While the Episcopal Church is becoming more diverse, the balance still tips strongly in one direction. The dark guest of that reality can color our perceptions of those unlike us, whether they be our priest or our parishioners.

Many would argue that the darkest guests are race, gender, and ethnicity. They may be right. When I was ordained a deacon in 1979, these dark guests were not mine to deal with personally, but over the course of the last three decades, being a white male has not proved to be the good-luck charm it once was. When I was first looking for a parish position, I was competing against other men—and mostly other white men. I was on the dominant side of the matter regarding race and gender when it came to priesthood in the Episcopal Church. Sadly, I observe that white candidates still often win out in this mostly white Episcopal Church. While it may be a disadvantage in some dioceses to be a male candidate, men still likely have the upper hand in most parish searches. While the ordination of women raised the intellectual and talent level of the priests in the Episcopal Church, at the same time, women have experienced a real glass ceiling in this church. I have concluded that it is easier for most women to become the Presiding Bishop or a seminary dean than rector of a well-resourced parish in the Episcopal Church. Do white men still have a certain edge in many parish searches? I think so. Too many women have been forced to take churches which many men would reject because of the economic challenges in those ministries. We still lack parity in salaries between men and women in the Episcopal Church. Gender inequality is certainly a dark guest for both men and women.

Race and ethnicity are equally troubling dark guests. Native Americans have worked hard to have a voice in the Episcopal Church. The Roman Catholic Church has grown stronger as Hispanic immigrants find a church home in their new country. The Episcopal Church has not done as good a job with non-white immigrants. Perhaps this is tied to classism and elitism. Suffice it to say: race, gender, and ethnicity can be dark guests for institutions and for us individually. Race, gender, and ethnicity can be barriers to positions, and they can have a limiting or even negative impact on our relationships with others in church and society. We are not color-blind yet. We still draw conclusions based on gender. We are not unaware of ethnic differences, or always able to celebrate and enjoy them.

The dark guest of sexuality comes calling often in our inner lives. The ambiguity and complexity of ourselves as sexual beings cannot be dismissed. We must be conversant with our sexual history and our attractions—or we will live dangerously close to the edge and risk those moments which can ruin the public life of ministry. There are far too many news stories of clerics accused of inappropriate sexual relations. Families and congregations are turned upside down as ordained leaders confront the turmoil that can be created when sexuality is unacknowledged. Could any of us survive such scrutiny—such analysis of the ways our public life matches or does not match our inner journey? Put the darkness, pain, conflict, and shadows of any of us in public view, and none of us would fare well.

Because of the dark guest of sexuality, many priests determine definite guidelines as they provide pastoral care. Boundaries are clearly identified. For example, priests do not meet for pastoral counseling with parishioners but a certain number of times; then, a referral is made to a respected professional in the community. A number of parishes have decided that office doors should have glass panels. While more open offices make sense, they do not resolve the issue. The dark guest of sexuality is not easily entertained. To say one must be disciplined is to deny the power of sexuality and the force of temptation. Is this more a problem for men than women? Perhaps—but sexual misconduct has also tarnished the short history of women in ordained ministry.

Priests, it is assumed, must be able to exegete Holy Scripture if they are to preach a convincing, compelling message. But perhaps of equal importance is the need for each priest to find a way to exegete his or her own story with a clear resolve. Such exegesis takes time, is often painful, and is never a work completed, but such exegesis or theological reflection precedes the possibility of living a balanced or peaceful life. I have come to terms with some of my dark guests, and therein I find some of the strength I need for the demands of a public, fishbowl priest-hood. But we must remember: coming to terms with a dark guest does not mean they leave your "house" of being.

For gays and lesbians, sexual orientation has become a dark guest for deployment in the Episcopal Church. Are more jobs open to heterosexuals? Yes, most definitely! I know of a well-qualified, very experienced gay priest who just completed five searches in which he made it to the final two or three under consideration. In each case, he was not hired. After the last search, he lamented the dark guest of sexuality as he tries to live into his priesthood. He said he was sure the parish he wanted to serve hired a "young white man with a wife, two children, and a station wagon." He is probably right. While we may say that the Episcopal Church is inclusive, we do not mean that "this job can be yours" applies to all applicants.

Careerism is a dark guest faced by both men and women priests. When I was ordained in 1979, it was assumed that a young white man with a good education would move from cu-rate to associate to rector—and maybe even to the episcopacy. There was a ladder to climb with appropriate career opportu-nities. I served as a curate for one year. The rector then named me his associate, a position I held for a little over a year. I be-came a rector of a thriving congregation when I was thirty-two years old—and left that post when I was forty-five years old. That was a long curacy at the Church of the Ascension in Hick-ory, North Carolina—almost fourteen years. I left my first rec-torship to become rector of the Church of the Redeemer in Baltimore—a much larger church in a much larger city. After five years, I joined the faculty of the Virginia Theological Sem-inary. Two of my three most immediate predecessors at Re-deemer left the parish to become bishops of North Carolina and Atlanta. My most immediate predecessor was in several bishop elections. When I went to Redeemer, Baltimore, I was aware of the career options it would afford me.

Careerism is often associated with ambition, even greed. Is that all bad? What is appropriate "drive" in ministry? How long is too long in a parish? Do we ever get a term of service

right? How much of the term of service is in our hands any-
way? Where is calling and vocation in the world of careerism,
ambition, and greed?

Fortunately or unfortunately, careerism is no longer a clear
path in the Episcopal Church. My three decades of priesthood
have been a time of institutional upheaval in our church, culture, and world. In the late 1970s, life in the Episcopal Church
was disrupted by a conflictive revision of the *Book of Common
Prayer*. The 1979 Prayer Book was preceded by the chaos of
the Vietnam War in the 1960s, and before that by the civil
rights movement in the 1950s and 1960s. Perhaps each decade
has its moments which rightly claim the church's attention.
Women's ordination to the priesthood was such a multi-decade
moment. The rights of gays and lesbians are still front and center. The ordination of women, gays, and lesbians has upset the
"apple cart" of traditional careerism. What was a typical path
for a young male ordinand does not seem to be the likely path
of a young female ordinand. Certainly the age at ordination
makes a difference in the career path. Gays and lesbians have
not found deployment easy—and often second and third jobs
with experience under their belt are as hard to find as the first
job out of seminary.

Changes in the Episcopal Church are rewriting career advancement. Also, unfavorable economic winds have complicated the job market. For example, there are fewer assistant or
associate positions in the Episcopal Church. An increasing number of seminarians leave their three years of residential formation and find themselves on their own, leading small
congregations as vicars, priests-in-charge, and even rectors,
often on a part-time basis. New mentoring models are emerging,
and all these changes are having an impact on career trajecto-
ries. Am I saying that the dark guest of careerism is dying? Perhaps—but another related dark guest will emerge. Will it be the
reality that full-time priesthood can no longer be a lifetime op-
tion in the Episcopal Church? Vocation or calling is no longer
tied so directly to adequate compensation. What will this mean
for recruitment and job satisfaction, or for a sense of call?

Finally, we return to the dark guest of human relationships. Family relationships take time, presence, and energy. As a young rector, I missed so much of my children's childhood. I was out almost every night "doing" church work. If I saw my wife and children at dinner, I was very lucky. When I finally got home, my young children were long asleep. Was it worth it? No. Of course, parishes do not employ us to be good fathers or mothers. They want us to work and to work hard—and to be an exemplary parent at the same time. Parishes want priests who produce—good sermons, sound budgets, amazing programs, and all the rest. How do you find the balance between family and the demands that are embedded in priesthood? This is a dark guest we must entertain.

Priestly ministry is in many ways a very delicate flower. It cannot survive outside of a loving community. The path to Holy Orders would have defeated me had it not been for family, mentors, and, in particular, my wife Linda. Indeed, putting on the habit of priesthood and living the craft of priesthood cannot be done without loving community.

My ordaining bishop told me that one cannot have friends in the parishes one serves. Impossible, I thought! And yet, he was probably right. To have a friend is to be blessed beyond words—but it does complicate life for the fishbowl priest. For me this was less a problem in a larger congregation—but still not uncomplicated. But can you go through life with only the friends you made before ordination? In deep human relationships outside of the family, it is clear that the personal life of the priest is always a very visible part of the priest's public life.

So, how do we attend to these dark, uninvited guests? How do we read or interpret the inner life which is so critical to the etiquette and ethics of a public life in the priesthood? We may not succeed if we take the inner journey unaccompanied. Spiritual directors and therapists are necessary companions when attending to dark guests or confronting darkness, pain, conflict, and shadows. The dark night is not bearable alone. Most of all, priests need their own carefully tended relationship with

God. So, a life of prayer becomes necessary for the priest's inner journey and his or her public service.

Attending to the dark guests has been part of what I will call the constant search for my authentic calling. The writer of the Revelation to John has a message for Ephesus: "But I have this against you, that you have abandoned the love you had at first" (Revelation 2:4). For me, I translate that to mean: I have abandoned the love I first had in ministry. I am constantly trying to recover the "first love" of vocation when it seemed so pure and God-centered. Ministry for me—and the dark guests have pulled me in this direction—has been a wandering from the authentic truth of my ordination day. The stuff of ministry often obscures the substance of ministry. I can no longer see clearly the moments of calling which prepared me for the craft of priesthood. Is there too much water over the dam? Have I spent too much time with the dark guests and not enough with myself or with God? I do think at times that the darkness has overcome the light in my practice of ministry. I do worry that serving God has been replaced with serving God's people. Can you love God and love the church at the same time? It is hard work being a priest. To persevere I have found that I must pray daily to recover the calling which I believe is mine to be a priest. Being a priest is never a passive vocation.

I draw strength from Hebrews 6:10–12, where I find that God "will not overlook your work and the love that you showed for his sake in serving the saints, as you still do." The writer of Hebrews begs us not to become "sluggish," but to be "imitators of those who through faith and patience inherit the promises." Read another way: Attend the dark guests but do not focus on them. Focus rather on God's promises and live by faith and with patience. Authentic, imperfect priesthood after the order of Melchizedek is a lifelong work, a vocation always coming into being and practice. As priests, we are always recovering the love we first had. We are always entertaining dark guests.

Chapter 11

A Holy Craft

Let your priests be clothed with righteousness.
(Psalm 132:9)

When I set out to write this book, I wanted to connect good priestly habits to thoughtful theological reflection. I wanted to connect etiquette to ethics, practice to theology. I treated my own priesthood as a case, using sermons and stories to recall the ways I have lived this craft which has been my life. The good priestly habits which I have suggested will not please everyone or fit all priests. There is no one size of priesthood. Some will say that this book is too subjective to be helpful. But I only have my vantage point, and I have tried to speak out of the integrity and richness of my experience.

I do care a great deal about the etiquette side of priesthood in the Episcopal Church. Outward appearances do matter: the way people present themselves, the homes in which they live and love, the places where people offer praise and worship, the appearance of the spaces where daily work happens, and the countless ways people relate to others. I have not plowed through my life for what could be labeled superficial reasons. After all, does it really matter if I pick up the wrong fork at a dinner party? Does it matter if I do not write thank you notes? Does it matter if I do not respond to emails? Does it matter if

I am always late? Does it really matter if I leave parties without thanking the hosts? Does it matter if I wear dirty liturgical vestments? Is it a sin to wear a stole that is off-center, hanging on my body lopsided? What's wrong with a little lace on my alb? Are polished shoes required? Does it matter if I let my hair down at a wedding reception and have a little too much to drink? Yes, it really matters how you look, what you do, and what you say. The medium and the message are bound together.

My priesthood has been a patchwork of pleasure, pain, promise, and privilege because the outward signs and symbols of my life have been in conversation with the interior commotion that goes to the heart of my identity. My interior life of thought, prayer, agony, and complexity has always been more active than my exterior life of actions, words, habits, and manners. My priesthood makes sense to me because I have been attentive to my whole being, the inner life and its outward manifestation. Several conclusions guide me as I reflect on priest as baptizer, presider and celebrant, preacher, teacher, officiant, pastor, administrator, leader, theologian, and practitioner.

First: *priesthood is sacramental.* The interiority of my life is mingled with and informs the external reality of my life. The outward and visible are deeply attached to the inward and invisible. In the blessed sacraments, the ordinary is changed—and yet it appears the same. Bread is prayed into the Body of Christ at the eucharistic table; yet, it is still bread. In Holy Baptism, water is sanctified by the power of the Holy Spirit and people are "cleansed from sin and born again," as the *Book of Common Prayer* puts it. We outwardly anoint the faithful with holy oil, as we believe there is "inward anointing of the Holy Spirit." At ordination, the bishop and faithful lay hands upon the head of the ordinand. In a bold moment, the bishop tells God: "Fill her with grace and power, and make her a priest in your Church." The person is changed, yet looks the same. Priesthood involves a sacramental transformation.

Ordination is a sacrament and priesthood is sacramental. In fact, that is true for the priesthood of all believers. Our priesthood, our vocations are sacramental—and are so by our baptisms. In the examination of the ordinand in the Prayer Book at a service of priesting, the bishop says: "All baptized people are called to make Christ known as Savior and Lord."[39] The priesthood of all believers is sacramental. Ordination to the priesthood is a particular sacrament, a certain gift, a unique calling, a sacred habit. Ordination or consecration is about being chosen by God and affirmed by God's church. Ordination to the priesthood is not about individual choosing or self-selection. Indeed, priesthood is transformative—because it is God's action in a particular person's life.

Second: *ordination to the priesthood does make the ordained different.* On the day of ordination, the priest does not enter a profession. The priest is invited into a way of being, indeed a way of life. I have been chosen and I am different—that is why it is so difficult. There is a particularity about priesthood which makes the person different. At the ordination of a priest, the *Book of Common Prayer* refers to the "consecration of the priest." To sanctify or to consecrate is to acknowledge a sacramental transformation and a difference: it is to set something or someone ordinary apart for a specific, often extraordinary, purpose. The priest, an ordinary man or woman, is made to be something very different. Ordination is a moment of ontological change. Our inner being is changed when holy hands are placed upon us. In the examination of ordinands for the priesthood and as the priest is set apart for service, the bishop is quick to say: "Now you are called to work as a pastor, priest, and teacher, together with your bishop and fellow presbyters, and to take your share in the councils of the Church."[40] Ordination to the priesthood made me different. It called forth and calls for a unique set of gifts, a particular set of skills. Ordination results in a different way of being, both outwardly and inwardly. Priests are not just like everybody else. There is a holy

---

39. *The Book of Common Prayer* (1979), 531.
40. *The Book of Common Prayer* (1979), 531.

life which is implied when one is consecrated for service as a priest.

Third: *the priest is different in and for the body of Christ.* The priest is not different for himself or herself. In the service for the Ordination of a Priest, after the ordinand is "made" a priest, the bishop continues: "May *he* exalt you, O Lord, in the midst of your people." *In the midst of your people.* Priests cannot live on pedestals—of their own making or on those made by others for them. The ordinand who becomes a priest is to "offer spiritual sacrifices" acceptable to God; to proclaim boldly the "gospel of salvation"; and to rightly administer "the sacraments of the New Covenant."[41] So, in a moment, the priest, as the Anglican Divine George Herbert puts it, who is "unfit for Holy Writ" becomes the proclaimer of the gospel and the bearer of the sacraments. The one who is a sacrament gives the sacraments to the people of God. Being different is about serving, not being served. Being different is about leading, proclaiming, bearing holy elements to holy people.

There is in serving a sacrificial side. This is the reason I find problematic so much of our talk about wellness, self-care, and boundaries. I do believe in taking care of myself—but I am quite weary of a preoccupation in ministry formation today which focuses excessively on wellness and self-care. Being different is about serving tirelessly in the church and in the world. Let us hear again the word from Ephesians: "Of this gospel I have become a servant according to the gift of God's grace that was given me by the working of God's power" (3:7). A person is made a priest for God and for God's community. When a man or woman becomes a priest, he or she becomes a servant. Ordination is not about self-realization. It is not about self-disclosure. It is not about self-discovery. It is not about self-care. Priesthood is about the fulfillment of God's will in a particular life and ministry. Priesthood is about living a mystery which is focused on the care of souls. Priesthood is about the transformation of the self—but it is not about the self. Priesthood can never be about personal success. It is about emptying ourselves,

---

41. *The Book of Common Prayer* (1979), 533–534.

not about climbing the corporate ladder of a profession. "Let him who boasts, boast of the Lord" (1 Corinthians 1:31).

Fourth: *ordination calls out of a person a new life,* which involves a new way of being, a new set of practices, new habits, even a new habit or way of dressing. A priest is made for the "household of God," which is "built upon the foundation of the apostles and prophets, with Christ Jesus himself as the cornerstone." The priest is a vicar of Christ, and the gospel message must be conveyed by the messenger to the church and the world with as few obstacles or impediments as possible. The priest is not a self-centered representative; ordination is not about telling my story over and over again. It is about bearing in our being the Word that is made flesh in Jesus Christ. The content of the priest's life should not be different from the character of the priest's life. The ethics of priesthood are evidenced in the etiquette of priesthood; and the etiquette or habits of priesthood evolve from the ethics, the theological core where we grow with God day by day. Theology shapes practice, practice shapes theology—and the craft of priesthood claims the life of one who is made a priest for the church and for the world, chosen by God and God's church.

My conclusions—the sacrament of priesthood, the difference of priesthood, the relationship of priesthood to the church, and the new life or demands of priesthood—are not very realistic. These conclusions are certainly not practical. I was chosen and made a priest on May 3, 1980 in the Diocese of Western North Carolina. But since that day, I have touched the bread and poured the wine with soiled hands. Too many times I have enjoyed the privilege of priesthood and benefited wrongly from the difference of priesthood. I have not worn the towel of servanthood with much grace and consistency. The habit of my priesthood has been worn by a flawed character "unfit for holy writ." Being made a priest has been for me an ongoing invitation to grow—awkwardly and sometimes creatively—with my own complexity, my own ambiguity, my own memoir of sadness and happiness. I think I can say that I have stepped in and out of my priesthood, the very priesthood that has become my life.

Temptations of ministry

In a chapter in his book *Freedom for Ministry* called "The Pursuit of Holiness," Richard John Neuhaus considers the challenges or "temptations of Christian ministry" which can undermine the "pursuit of holiness." His approach is strangely and deeply biblical: look at your weakness and find therein your strength. The one who seeks to be "an exemplary person" in priesthood faces strong contrary currents, and Neuhaus identifies them well: "activism, ambition, sexuality, and money." I want to spend some time on these—for I neglected to do so in 1979 as I prepared for ordination.

Neuhaus decides that activism is a "form of decadence."[42] I am decadent. So much of my ministry has been a busyness about many things. When I was ordained in 1979, it was not uncommon for a priest to work out of his "study." In fact, at Trinity Church in Asheville, my first workplace as a priest was a wormy chestnut-paneled "study." It had ample book shelves and suggested that therein a person thought, wrote, and prepared to meet God's people at God's altar week after week. When I left Asheville in 1981, I went to Ascension, Hickory and occupied an "office." This was more than a nomenclature shift. As rector of a growing congregation, there were many expectations and goals to be met. The rectory had a "study," but when I was at the church, my office door was open and I spent much of my time as an administrator, meeting people and chairing meetings. I remember that it was said that my predecessor at Ascension spent very little time in his office. That was seen as a virtue because he was out and about, calling on people and being a full-time pastor. In fact, his wife accompanied him on many of these pastoral visits. As the congregation grew and became more complex, being in the office was required, if not a necessity.

When I went to the Church of the Redeemer in 1995, I inhabited a large office with high windows. I often described it as my tree-house office. In the old part of the parish building,

---

42. Richard John Neuhaus, *Freedom for Ministry* (New York: Harper & Row, 1979), 200.

there was a paneled study where my predecessors kept most of their books and prepared their sermons. Still, it was the office that was the primary workplace for Redeemer's rector.

Activism takes its toll on the spiritual life, and it can never be the way to deal with the drabness, routine, and monotony of ministry. The empty well of ministry starts with the slow leaks of activism. Priests resent the old saw that we really only work one day a week. Activism may be overcompensating for the temptation of seeing priesthood as primarily Sunday work. Most priests are too busy to think. Most priests are too active to read. There is some truth to the old adage that you can look at the priest's bookshelves and determine the year he graduated from seminary. As I reread my sermons as part of writing this book, I saw the impact of activism on the quality of my writing and the depth of my thinking. Activism can breed a certain shallowness in ministry, a certain way of living on the surface and going through the motions.

Confronting the "decadence" of activism should not lead us to the conclusion that the antidote is self-care. The best way to deal with activism is to reflect theologically on ministry. Take time to search for God's presence in the busyness of priesthood. That search is at the core of what Neuhaus means by the "pursuit of holiness."

A second temptation for priests is ambition. Neuhaus knows that the "pursuit of holiness" requires a singleness of heart, a focus that is always larger than the self. He says that "the corruption of the present-day Church would be greatly reduced were more of its leaders compelled to office by obedience rather than attracted to office by ambition."[43] Perhaps this is easier said than done. Is ambition in and of itself bad? Is it a temptation that has no redeeming qualities? As a newly-minted priest, I was quite ambitious. Before the ink of my ordination certificate was dry, I wanted to be a rector. Why, I will never know. As a rector, I was quite ambitious for myself and my parish. I wanted the parish to grow. I wanted the budget to in-

---

43. Neuhaus, *Freedom for Ministry*, 213.

crease. I wanted the outreach to matter. I wanted the building to be more beautiful. I wanted many things.

While at the Church of the Redeemer, I became ambitious about ministry in the larger church. My involvement at Kanuga Conferences, Inc. intensified, and I enjoyed my role on the board of directors. I accepted an invitation to be on the board of Episcopal Relief and Development. While diocesan leadership was important to me at Ascension, the national church became my focus while in Baltimore. Was this ambition? Probably so! I plead guilty.

In my students at Virginia Theological Seminary, I look for a healthy dose of ambition. We should want to be the best priests possible. We should have goals and be focused on what we must do to realize those goals. At the same time, priesthood is not about success. Priesthood is more about mystery than achievement. It may be helpful to consider ambition as part of the community context which is ministry as a priest. What does it mean to be a leader who is ambitious in the midst of the people of God? Ambitious for what and for whom? Ambition can lead to pretension and the quest for power. But ambition can also lead to ministry results and doing good for the sake of the kingdom.

Not surprisingly, Neuhaus includes sexuality as a temptation. However, it should not be missed that the temptation for him is sexuality, not sex. For most of my years of ministry, human sexuality has been on the front burner of the Episcopal Church. In the 1970s, when people were honest they connected opposition to women priests to concerns about sexuality. By the same token, gay rights is about the challenge and complexity of human sexuality. As Neuhaus foretold, "fidelity, homosexuality, changing sex roles, marriage and celibacy—all are questions that will continue to claim the attention of the churches."[44] That's an understatement when it comes to the Episcopal Church of the last thirty years! But how do priests serve in the midst of such attention to sexuality? I think this is a very difficult assignment. On the one hand, a priest must live

---

44. Neuhaus, *Freedom for Ministry*, 225.

within his or her own being with the ambiguities and complexities that accompany our own sexuality. Being ordained does not negate our sexuality. Indeed, ordination confirms and celebrates who we are as beloved children of God. If priesthood is sacramental, then we must not pretend that we are not sexual beings. The whole of our being is God's gift, and sexuality is a temptation because of its mystery and complexity. This is true for all human beings, not just priests.

The priest as sexual being also lives a public life. In preaching and teaching, the priest is called upon to provide insights or to make pronouncements about sexuality, even as he or she struggles in private with the same. In all the commotion about sexuality, where is the priest's reasonable, thoughtful voice?

Neuhaus may be right: priests pledge to live exemplary lives. But with each of these temptations—activism, ambition, and sexuality—it is important to remember that the exemplary life is in constant need of amendment, forgiveness, and grace. The "pursuit of holiness" requires obedience to the One who is our Exemplar, Jesus Christ himself. Obedience is always an incomplete act, for we always live in tension with our limits. So, our "freedom for ministry" or freedom in life is never quite realized. Yes, even the priest is held captive and blessed at the same time by the fullness of humanity.

Neuhaus has strong words about money, his last temptation. He is intrigued about the ways we interpret the admonition in 1 Timothy 3 that a bishop should not be "a lover of money." Does that mean that ordination as an Episcopal priest includes a vow of poverty? Is the "good" priest the one who lives with little? When we say that the priesthood makes us different, does it mean automatically that we who are priests should be poor?

My students often bring me their first job descriptions and financial contracts. We look at the compensation and discuss the "temptation" of money. Is there ever enough? What does it mean to be "fairly compensated"? What is an appropriate lifestyle for the priest? Over time, I have concluded that money is not as great a temptation as is consumerism. Consuming more and more things and stuff has been more of a temptation for me than money itself. So, priests should be mindful of what they consume and what this means in terms of a particular, or even exemplary, lifestyle. Finally, there is something to be said for modesty when it comes to money. Modesty begets simplicity and that is good. Priests should be self-aware when it comes to what they wear, what they drive, and where they live. A disciplined priest makes decisions carefully and thoughtfully. Money can get priests in trouble. But lifestyle choices are a bigger temptation as priests are paid better than ever.

Walking through these great temptations—activism, ambition, sexuality, and money—provides me with an abiding realism about the craft of priesthood. Perhaps the one temptation that Neuhaus should have included is the grave danger that priests, in their care of souls, neglect their own souls. Such is the great peril of priesthood. For certain, I am not talking about self-care! Rather, I am struggling with the ways one leads an exemplary life or the ways one follows the Exemplar in that life which pursues holiness. How do you live the craft of priesthood and care for your soul? If the psalmist is right, how is the priest clothed with righteousness?

At some deep place, I know that priesthood is about my whole life, and about that whole life offered up to God in service and prayer. Most of this book has been about service, that wonderful and sacred mingling of etiquette and ethics. What I say and do matters as much as what I think and believe. I look into the mirror before a service of worship, not to see myself but to see Christ. I look into the mirror practically to be sure that my stole is properly placed, that my hair is combed, and that I look as presentable as possible. My concern about my appearance is not about me! I am concerned with how I appear because I do not want to draw attention to myself. It is the message that counts—but, Lord knows, the messenger can often get in the way of the message. People can miss the ethics of your message because the etiquette of your manners speaks so loudly!

But you can work forever and not get right the balance between etiquettes and ethics. Finally, priesthood is God's gift,
not a task. You can develop skills that will help you with the
craft, but priesthood is ultimately lived, not learned. Living
priesthood for me is more about prayer than service, more
about my relationship with God than the ministry which is
mine. I have not come to this conclusion overnight. I have arrived at the importance of informal, constant prayer because
my priesthood has, quite frankly, driven me to my knees on too
many occasions.

Prayer has worked for me because it is an effective way for
me to step out of my worldly-grounded life. I am a material
person, one who cares too much about art and beauty, nature
and buildings, this world and not the next. Prayer focuses my
aesthetic sensibilities and gives me the possibility of a right per-
spective. I suppose I am a praying aesthete—one who hungers
for God even as I fully embrace the beauty of this world and
the art of being human. The priest who is a praying aesthete
thirsts for God. In "Thirst," the epilogue to her moving book
of poems by the same name, Mary Oliver writes:

> Another morning and I wake with thirst for the goodness I
> do not have. I walk out to the pond and all the way God
> has given us such beautiful lessons. Oh Lord, I was never a
> quick scholar but sulked and hunched over my books past
> the hour and the bell; grant me, in your mercy, a little more
> time. Love for the earth and love for you are having such a
> long conversation in my heart. Who knows what will fi-
> nally happen or where I will be sent, yet already I have
> given a great many things away, expecting to be told to
> pack nothing, except the prayers which, with this thirst, I
> am slowly learning.[45]

That says it well for me: "Love for the earth and love for you
(God)." That's a translation of priest as praying aesthete. I have
strong artistic sensibilities that inform my etiquette, my manners. But my love for the beauty of the earth derives from my

---

45. Mary Oliver, "Thirst," in *Thirst: Poems* (Boston: Beacon Press, 2004),
69. Used by permission.

love and longing for God, hence the "long conversation in my heart" with God.

Indeed, it is to the poets that I run when I come to my last words about living the craft of priesthood. Words are very much part of my aesthetic sensibility. Mary Oliver's wisdom about packing nothing but her prayers for the journey is an insight I treasure. Priesthood is a lonely craft and is lived far from home. No place of ministry is ever home for the priest. If we are praying aesthetes, we are also, to use a more conventional phrase, praying pilgrims, wayfarers who serve without the comforts of home and hearth. The priest always lives in temporary quarters. The priest serves for a season in a place but not forever. If the priest in prayer does not live with God, the priest lives with no one.

The dour Welsh poet R. S. Thomas wrote a poem about these things. In "The Priest," Thomas laments:

> The priest picks his way
> Through the parish. Eyes watch him
> From windows, from the farms;
> Hearts wanting him to come near.
> The flesh rejects him.

Yes, the priest is different and rejection is part of living this craft. Rejection is at the heart of Christ's priesthood, as it was the story of Jesus' earthly life. The priest is Christ's icon, Christ's vicar—but priests and the people of God adjust constantly to the frailty of priesthood and the imperfection of the church. Thomas continues:

> Priests have a long way to go.
> The people wait for them to come
> To them over the broken glass
> Of their vows.

The "broken glass of their vows": that says beautifully what I referred to as stepping in and out of my vows. The "broken glass of their vows" provides an apt image of the imperfection of this pursuit which is priesthood. We never get the limits

right; the obedience is never constant; and the "freedom for
ministry" is never fully realized. The praying aesthete serves
with limited vision and makes many mistakes in living the craft.
R. S. Thomas concludes:

> "Crippled soul," do you say? looking at him
> From the mind's height; "limping through life
> On his prayers. There are other people
> In the world, sitting at table
> Contented, though the broken body
> And the shed blood are not on the menu."[46]

As a praying aesthete—as one who prays while loving the
beauty of the earth—I have "limped through life" on my
prayers. God called a "crippled soul" when God called me.
God called a human being who has served by God's grace
through the "broken glass" of my vows. Living the craft of
priesthood does not require an exemplary life. Living the craft
of priesthood requires a person who follows as faithfully as
possible the Exemplar, Jesus Christ, who is our great high
priest. A priest must pray constantly and love boldly this earth
and all its creatures.

Thomas is so right. Priests preside at altars of sacrifice and
victory. If the "broken body and the shed blood" of Jesus are
"on the menu," then priesthood will always be about rejection,
suffering, and the emptying of one's self. Living such a priesthood is also about dying to self and living more and more to
the God we know in Jesus Christ. Priests preside at a holy sacrifice time and time again, even as their lives are a living sacrifice for the One who has gone before us and who prepares a
place for us that is green and fertile for eternity. Such a holy
craft has been worth my life.

---

46. R. S. Thomas, "The Priest," in *Not That He Brought Flowers* (London:
Hart-Davis, 1968), 29. Used by permission.